ONE TEACHER'S CLASSROOM

Strategies for Successful Teaching and Learning

Dale Gordon

ELEANOR CURTAIN
PUBLISHING

First published in 1992
ELEANOR CURTAIN PUBLISHING
906 Malvern Road
Armadale 3143
Australia

Copyright © Dale Gordon 1992

National Library of Australia
Cataloguing-in-publication data:

Gordon, Dale.
   One teacher's classroom: successful strategies
   for teaching and learning.
   ISBN 1 875327 15 0.

   1. Primary school teaching. I. Title.

371.102

Production by Sylvana Scannapiego,
   Island Graphics
Edited by Ruth Siems
Text design by Sarn Potter
Cover design by David Constable
Cover photographs by Sara Curtain
Typeset in 12/14 Baskerville by Optima Typesetting
   and Design, Melbourne
Printed in Australia by Impact Printing

CONTENTS

133371

INTRODUCTION

LOOKING AT THE THEORIES BEHIND THE PRACTICE

It is very difficult for teachers to put into words the theories on which they base their teaching practice. I have been struggling to describe my philosophical base to myself for years.

However, once a philosophical base is defined, it becomes easier to institute teaching practices that are aligned to it, and to provide the learning environment that you want for learners in your classroom.

It is when I take a look at my own learning, confirm in my own mind how I think I learn best and, perhaps, isolate the factors that cause me to learn, that I can begin to make statements about my philosophy of teaching and learning. Then I can begin to apply this philosophy to my teaching and learning practice, and use it as a basis for doing certain things and not doing others in my classroom. I must ask myself:

- what have I learnt quickly
- what I have learnt easily and effectively
- what helped me to do it.

A TRUE CONFESSION: A TIME I LEARNT SOMETHING

All my life I had avoided learning to sew. Sewing cards, sewing kits, sewing baskets regularly appeared in my stocking at Christmas, but I ignored them: I much preferred to do anything else at all!

When I was about ten, I succumbed to my younger sister's pleas to make some clothes for her dolls. I raided boxes of fabrics and trimmings carefully stored for years by my mother against the coming of another depression. I commandeered her Singer sewing machine, and waved aside offers of help from my grandmother. My sister watched, awestruck and nervous, as I imperiously ruined beautiful laces and braids, cut up fine old woollens and organdies and so tangled the Singer that I was never allowed to use it again. My mother was beyond fury when she arrived at the scene, and the 'dolls' clothes' were appalling. Within days they had fallen to pieces in the bottom of toy boxes and under beds.

After that I gave up sewing until I was in Year 7, when needlecraft was compulsory for all girls at our local secondary school. It was expected that we would make a collection of sewing samplers. We were given squares of fabric on which we were to demonstrate our mastery of different sewing techniques — hemming, buttonholing, 'lazy daisy' stitching, tacking, cross-stitching; an endless repertoire was to be catalogued in our sampler collection. I couldn't do any of them, I hated it, and I put the whole lot in a shoe box under my bed and forgot it. The weekend before our samplers were to be handed in, I prevailed upon my grandmother to sew mine for me. She sat and finished them all in one evening.

My next trial did not come until I was at teachers' college. As part of the art/craft assessment we had to sew a 'garment suitable for our personal use'. My best friend, a straight 'A' needlework student agreed to make my garment, a hideous brown checked dress, in return for a two-thousand-word essay on speech training methods for the articulatory impaired. I was spared yet again.

It was not until I was married that I finally learned to sew.

I became pregnant, and realised that we could not afford to buy the clothes we needed for the baby, or for the growing me! I explored possibilities and, after a couple of months when things started to get desperate, it began to dawn on me that the one feasible way out was to make the necessary items myself.

Now, of course, I had a real reason for sewing. I could see the purpose for it right there before my eyes. I needed maternity and baby clothes, baby linen and nursery drapes. I decided to have a go.

Completely ignoring my personal history of ineptitude, I bought a cheap sewing machine, searched the markets for fabric offcuts, scraps and 'job lots' of trimmings and haberdashery, decoded paper patterns and began to sew.

I couldn't be stopped. I sewed night and day. Fabrics, paper patterns, ribbons and laces covered the house. I was fortunate to have a good friend, who was prepared to show me what to do next, and to rethread my sewing machine every time I got it completely choked up.

Response to my sewing was immediate. I wasted no time in showing off my creations to a very appreciative audience, my husband, who was more than delighted to realise that a thrifty needlecraft genius had lain dormant under the facade of incompetence with which he was familiar.

Of course I made mistakes. I spent a lot of time unpicking and resewing tiny seams on tiny garments. It took me a very long time to even master the straight hem. I threw away some of my more spectacular mistakes. But as the raw materials were the cheapest in town, I did not feel too guilty about this and, naturally, I didn't tell many people about this part of the process.

One day, as I was admiring my collection of tiny lace-trimmed and embroidered baby clothes, I realised that I was having a good time — I *loved* sewing, and... I was quite competent as well. It was a revelation.

BUILDING A PHILOSOPHY

It is evident, from reflecting on this chronicle, that at that time I was a very 'immersed' learner, with a very long list of reasons why this was so.

- I was ready, willing and able.
- I was completely involved in the task.
- I began with confidence. I knew I could do it. I bought the sewing machine, the fabrics, the patterns without doubt even crossing my mind. After all, all females could sew, couldn't they? What, in the culture of the time, would have me believe otherwise?

Of course, despite these positive attitudes to sewing, I needed and luckily received a lot of practical help as well.

- I had a friend who was prepared to show me what to do when I needed help.
- I learnt a lot from 'having a go' and I made lots of mistakes.
- I had the resources I needed to do the sewing.
- It was up to me to make all the decisions about the task: I had sole responsibility for choosing what to do, for deciding when I did it, and how much of it I did.
- I had plenty of time.
- I had a real reason to do it.
- I had very supportive feedback. My friend gave me constructive and helpful advice, and my husband gave me praise. He showed his confidence in my ability to sew by asking me to do other sewing jobs, like mending and repairing other clothes.

TRANSLATING THE PHILOSOPHY INTO PRACTICE

When I have a clear mental picture of how I learnt to sew, and can start to isolate the factors that contributed to my success, I can begin to examine my role as teacher. I can make some statements about how I want to teach based on my experiences as a learner and I can say: 'I want to teach this way, because this is how learners learn.'

I can say:

1   I will show children what I do to learn — I will demonstrate my learning because learners need to see how it is done.

Therefore, I will show children how I write by telling them what I am thinking as they watch me write.

2   I will make sure that materials and resources are always available and easily accessible so that children can use them freely and without interruption to their work. Learners must have the resources they need to learn when they need them.

Therefore, all publishing materials will be kept on a trolley, and not in the storeroom cupboard.

3   I will be available to support children in their learning, when it is important to give them help.

Therefore I will be available to discuss children's work with them, even if it's lunchtime.

4   I will allow children plenty of time in which to learn and in which to practice what they learn because learning needs time and practice.

Therefore, we will all read every day.

5   I will always remember that every learner is different. They will learn different things at different rates.

Therefore, I will monitor each child's learning and make decisions about each one individually.

6   I will allow children to choose what they need to learn because *need* determines successful learning.

Therefore, I will plan the learning programs with the children in order to meet their needs.

7   I will always let children know that I expect them to learn because I believe they can. If learners really believe they can do it, they are prepared to 'have a go'.

Therefore, I will always look at achievements, not failures. I will plan activities to boost children's self-esteem. I will help children to define their own expectations for themselves.

8   I know that learners make mistakes, and that analysing mistakes helps them to develop better strategies for the next attempt.

Therefore, I will praise attempts at spelling, and make children aware of which of their strategies were successful and which were not.

9   I will be an aware and supportive audience for each child. I will be ready to respond positively and as appropriately as I can to their learning needs. Learners need to know how others think they are going.

Therefore, classroom conferences of all types will be held every day, and I will listen first!

IMPLICATIONS FOR CLASSROOM PRACTICE

As I look at these statements about learning that underpin my teaching practice, I can see that they are all interrelated. In order to provide for one, the others need to be in place. For example, if I want children to develop their reading skills they must have plenty of time to read every day. In order to have children read every day the children themselves must *want* to read every day, and for this to happen they must feel confident about their reading, and motivated to do it.

Therefore, I need to put all my other statements about learning into practice, so that children will feel motivated to read, and confident that they can read.

• I must demonstrate how a reader reads, by reading with them, so that children will see what to do.

• I must provide resources, so there is plenty of easily accessible reading material.

• I must help children learn to read. Therefore, the daily reading sessions must be backed up with plenty of other reading experiences which have targeted individual children's learning to read needs.

• I realise that every learner is different, so I need to provide for this. I must ensure that there is an enormous range of reading materials in the classroom to cater for individual differences. I need to provide choices of places for reading: easy chairs, floor space, cosy corners, outdoor areas, desks. I need to provide time that is flexible in length.

• The children must be free to select their own reading materials, because learners learn best when they choose what they do. I must allow time for children to choose what they want to read, and I must show them how a reader chooses what to read.

• I will look around the children, and expect that they will all be reading, even on their first day at school.

• I will be aware that children may not read accurately, and that the mistakes that occur are a natural part of learning to read.

• I will discuss and share children's reading with them, responding to their pleasures and disappointments about their reading in ways that will lead them to continue to read.

What if I change one part of this activity? For example, if I decide not to read myself, but to use the time while the children are reading to file away some of the papers from my desk — if I take the attitude that I can read any time, but I've got to get this cleared before the end of the day. What is lost?

Instead of demonstrating how a reader reads, I am letting children know that:

1   This time is too valuable for me to spend it reading.
2   Filing is more important to me.
3   Reading is something to do when there is nothing else to do.
4   It's okay for you children to read, you have nothing else to do.
5   This time is for other activities as well as reading.
6   Do as I say, not as I do.

What could be children's possible responses? Maybe these:

1   If she's not going to read then I'm going to sort my footy cards.
2   This time is not special, I'll just ask if I can go to the toilet. I want to check out what they're doing in the next classroom.
3   She's preparing for the rest of the day; so can I. I'll just sharpen my pencils.
4   We can do what we like as long as we are quiet so that the teacher can get on with her work.
5   The teacher doesn't like to read so it doesn't matter if I don't like to read. It can't be that important.
6   Reading is not as important as cleaning up.
7   You don't have to read every day when you grow up, why bother now?

See what happened! I have devalued reading by demonstrating that I do not consider it to be an important enough activity for me to do. All the other provisions I have made to encourage children to want to read have become meaningless. Why provide a wide variety of reading materials if reading is not important? Why set aside a special time? Why engage in other reading activities planned to develop reading strategies if learning to read is not important? Why bother to discuss what has been read after the reading sessions? It doesn't matter what you did during the reading session.

The message is clear. Everything that happens in the classroom has an impact on what else happens. Teaching is like a house of cards: take away one part and the whole structure collapses. The teacher must always look for the effect that each part of teaching and learning practice has on other parts.

I always keep in mind the factors that help me learn best. Then, when I am teaching, I can ask myself, is this classroom activity going to help children to learn? How would it help me to learn? If I cannot justify the activity by saying how it will help, then why am I doing it?

PART ONE

CREATING A LEARNING ENVIRONMENT

I want children to learn in my classroom. I know, therefore, that I have a responsibility to plan and maintain a learning environment that will support the children as they learn.

It is not a straightforward or simple responsibility. First, I have to be clear about what is needed in an environment to support learning. What do I, as a learner, need to learn? Knowing what *I* need will help me to understand the learning needs of others and to provide for them.

I remember a time when my daughter, then aged eight, came home from ballet school with four small pieces of fluorescent pink lycra fabric, six metres of tulle netting and 350 sequins and announced that I had to assemble these into a go-go dancer's outfit for the end of the year concert, and preferably to have it ready by next Wednesday when rehearsals started. There were no written instructions. My daughter gave me a vague but enthusiastic description of how fantastic the completed garment should look.

What did I need in my environment to even begin this daunting task? I worked out that there were three basic essentials:

1   **Time**, and long stretches of it, without interruptions, to work out what to do and then to do it — there were 350 sequins, remember.

2   **A place**, especially organised for my purpose, with a bench where I could set up my fabric and sequins in the right order and leave them there between sessions, safely away from the rest of the household chaos.

3   **Resources**, particularly suited to the task, like my sewing machine with its stretch fabric overlocker, plus scissors, pins, etc., and a large cushion to muffle my screams when things went wrong.

So, when planning my classroom, I think of these three things:

Time

Will the children have the time they need to learn?

Place

Is the classroom organised to suit the learning activities that are to take place?

Resources

Will the resources that are needed be there? Are they easily accessible to the children who need them? Are they the most suitable for the activities for which they are to be used?

1

PROVIDING TIME

Despite the restrictions imposed by the school timetable, it is possible to develop a timetable that will give children the blocks of time they need for their learning.

Remember the 'good old days', when timetabling was a mathematical exercise? We juggled subjects to fit the mystical departmental time allocations for each subject: it was a nightmare. Imagine juggling with constraints like,

> *Forty-seven and a half minutes a week for health and hygiene; will that leave me enough time for the three and three-quarter hours I have to 'do' maths in, twenty-five and a half hours minus three and three-quarters leaves...word study has to have two and a half hours, creative writing has one and a half hours...*

These days I try to avoid specific time allocations for specific subjects:
* I want the class time to be flexible, and used to provide for and respond to children's needs and purposes as they become apparent.
* I want children to know that they have lots of time to consolidate their learning.
* I want the children to see their learning in holistic ways, with no artificial subject 'compartments'. The tasks children are engaged in need to be integrated into whole learning experiences.

I need open-ended time blocks if these objectives are to be met, and the children need to know that their class time is planned to allow for these, so they can relax and learn at a pace that suits each of them.

YEAR 3/4				
MONDAY	TUESDAY	WEDNESDAY	THURSDAY	FRIDAY
Language →			*Religious instruction (specialist)	
RECESS				
Maths	Art/craft (specialist)	Maths	Library (specialist)	Maths
LUNCH				
Uninterrupted, sustained, silent reading				
Inquiries		Physical education		Cleaning up
RECESS				
Italian (specialist)	Inquiries →			Sport

Year 3/4 timetable

When I am preparing the yearly timetable, mostly in discussion with the children who will be guided by it, I write in the non-negotiable time slots first: sport, art/craft sessions in the art room, community language sessions, etc. Then I consider what time blocks are left. With a Year 3/4 class, I wrote in only four other areas of study after the non-negotiable specialist sessions were filled — maths, language, inquiries, and uninterrupted, sustained, silent reading (USSR).

With a Year 6 class, my timetable developed extra dimensions, allowing time at the beginning of each week to discuss expectations for the week, and time at the end to reflect on the week's activities, to review, and then preview activities to come. Apart from the specialist teachers' time slots, only USSR remains as a timetabled activity.

Once the timetable is established, I structure learning sessions within each time block, and I make sure children have time for the following:

1 A preview of the session, and expectations for it.
   Where and how does the work planned for this session fit into our broad picture?

2 A demonstration of the learning to be undertaken by the group, if this support is required and especially if new skills are involved.
   What do I do here? How?

3 Practice of the learning, with help if needed from other children, the teacher or anyone else in the room, e.g. parents, librarian.
   How am I going?

4 Sharing learning, ideas and opinions with others.

YEAR 6					
Per	MONDAY	TUESDAY	WEDNESDAY	THURSDAY	FRIDAY
1	Expectations/ preview			Christian education	
				Silent reading	
2				Italian (specialist)	
RECESS					
3		Music (specialist)		Activity maths (specialist)	Silent reading
4					Reflections on week, review
LUNCH					
5	Silent reading				Sport
6		Library (specialist)	Physical education (specialist)	Art (specialist)	

Year 6 timetable

I'm proud of this work.
What do you think of it so far?
Let me explain to you what I've done here.

5 Working in groups, peer tutoring, exchange of learning.
What did you do about this?
What strategies did you use?
Help me with my problem.

6 Reflecting on the learning, implications for the next session, and the next step.
Next time I need to...
Why did this happen?

This type of lesson structure will help me keep tabs on what each child is doing. I want to know how their work is progressing, how they feel about it, and what will they need in order to continue.

Therefore, I build in a lot of observation time for myself. At the end of each session I would plan to have at least a general idea of what each child has been doing. A typical session might, therefore, look like this:

Lesson structure

1   Initial whole class focus: preview the session, look at content of the session, what do we need for this session?
2   Individual work/teacher observing and conferencing.
3   Group activity/teacher observing and conferencing.
4   Conclusion: review the session, look at the products from the session, what do we need to do next session?

SAMPLE LESSON STRUCTURE
INITIAL WHOLE CLASS FOCUS

This would take about 15 minutes, and generally take place in the class meeting area. Particular objectives for the session might be listed for discussion, on a board, on paper.

The purpose for this initial time is to allow children to become completely familiar and comfortable with the activities they are to be involved in during the session. Every child must feel confident that they can meet the set expectations.

General plans for the session would be discussed. I would offer some broad advice and direction, remind children of where this session fitted into 'the big picture' and what was expected of them. Children would be asked to participate in this discussion, offering their advice and opinion on the direction of the session.

Specific plans for the session would then be discussed from the list. Ideas, suggestions, potential problems, and strategies to solve them would be aired. A whole range of issues might be aired at this time, for example:

- We might discuss a skill or strategy that children will need to employ to perform activities during the session, e.g. what are the criteria for deciding when to start new paragraphs?
- We might listen to and list ideas for extensions to the session's activities, e.g. when all children complete their book reviews, should the reviews be collated and made into a classroom resource, or put in the library for general use by the whole school? Should they be bound into a book, or should each review be attached to the book it reviewed?
- I might demonstrate how to do something that children will be doing during the session, e.g. how to use the spelling check on the computer, how to use a thesaurus.
- We might read a shared book, to look at how other authors write.

INDIVIDUAL LEARNING/TEACHER CONFERENCING

Maybe 30–40 minutes would be available here. This is the 'heads down tails up' part of the session with children working mainly on individual tasks. I am busy too, meeting with children, checking progress and performance. I use a variety of conferencing techniques during this time to ensure that I know what is happening with each child. Conferencing as a means of feedback and assessment is also discussed in chapter ten.

ROVING CONFERENCE

This is the quick check. Is everyone on task? If not, why not, and what can be done to help? What immediate help is needed — organising space, materials, reworking task goals, setting up a peer support group? This roving conference might be done one or two times a session, and **always** at the beginning, to ensure that all children start well.

SMALL GROUP CONFERENCE

At the beginning of the year the class is grouped into a number of small 'conference' groups. Group membership is decided randomly, and remains constant for the year. The day of the week each group meets with me is also constant. This means that children always know when their group meets. They can become comfortable with the routine of being prepared to report on their work.

During the conference session I write down, in my observation diary (see part four) a brief word or two about what each child is presently working on, what plans they have for the immediate future of their work, and what needs they might have for it. This information will feed into program planning for that child.

The children can seek advice, opinion and help from the members of their group, including me. Because of the regularity of the meeting and the constant membership, children become very familiar with each other's work, and can offer informed advice and opinion based on that familiarity.

INDIVIDUAL CONFERENCE

This is the 'in-depth' look at a child's work, and in a typical session I would only have time for one, maybe two such conferences. Children put their names on a waiting list for an individual conference, and if there is a backlog of people waiting I use any time throughout the day to confer with children. See part four for more details of these conferences.

'STRIKE WHILE THE IRON IS HOT' CONFERENCES

During the session I might observe a child struggling with some aspect of the work and decide that intervention will give the support needed for the child to proceed. So I help them: 'Try this', 'This might be what you are trying to do', 'Have a look at this, it's like yours, and it might help you.'

SHARING CONFERENCES

We usually have these at the end of this part of the session. They are planned to exchange information about what has been happening during the session.

- What have you learned/achieved?
- What do you think should happen next?
- Who has some advice, or an opinion to offer?

GROUP ACTIVITIES, GROUP TEACHING/CONFERENCING

This part of the session would take about 20 minutes. Activities will usually be child initiated, in that children will be pursuing the goals they have set for their working group of the moment. Their activities might include group publishing, playwriting and producing, group research, peer tutoring.

During this time I might hold support sessions for groups of children. These groups might be composed of children who have common needs that I have observed during conferences, for example, children who misread instructions, or who are struggling with the use of apostrophes. I might also announce that I am holding a workshop related to children's present tasks, for example, how to use a street directory, or set out a playscript. Anyone can attend these workshops.

CONCLUSION

This takes about 15 minutes and is a reviewing time when children can appraise their work, reflect on it, recap and report on it. Activities might include reading from the session's products, serial reading, celebrating achievement, discussing problems that have arisen, and looking for possible solutions.

Finally, we would preview the next session, looking at future plans for individual, group and whole class work.

2

PROVIDING A PLACE

If I expect children to adopt an approach to their learning that will enable them to work independently and with confidence, I must make sure they have a suitable working environment. It must be obvious that their environment is planned to suit their needs, and the needs of the tasks.

The classroom layout must reflect my expectation of how I think learning will occur.

- If I expect children to work in independent groups, I group their worktables for this purpose, not in fixed rows.
- If I expect children to research writing topics, I bring the books needed into the room, I don't leave them in the library, or expect they will be packed away at the end of each session.
- If I expect children to write, I provide areas for each part of the writing process — pre-planning, drafting, publishing, sharing.
- If I expect children to read silently for a sustained period, I make sure there are inviting (and good) books about, and comfortable places to sit and read.
- If I expect the children to take responsibility for their learning, where's my table?

If I am placed at the front, facing the children and next to the blackboard where I can keep an eye on all the action, what message am I giving to these children about becoming independent and responsible learners? Certainly not that I trust them to work independently.

My desk needs to be situated to suit *my work too*. I must demonstrate that the classroom is my workplace and that my working conditions are as suitable for my work as I can make them.

Two useful classroom layouts I have used, and that are functional for all year levels, are detailed here. Plan one is for a conventionally designed classroom — a basic square — and plan two is for a room with a more flexible and exciting design.

In both these plans the layout provides plenty of working areas for the writer.

- **For planning writing:** a library area, reference shelves for information and research, group tables, discussion areas, open floor space for sharing ideas
- **For drafting writing:** computers, corral style tables for uninterrupted individual writing (these are usually facing walls so that children can work without being distracted by other activity around them), group tables, open areas for group drafts
- **For conferencing writing:** quiet areas, away from work tables, the teacher's work area
- **For publishing writing:** group tables for large pieces of work and group publishing, typewriters, computers, easy access to bookmaking materials, papers, art materials.
- **For sharing and celebrating writing achievements:** an open floor space that will seat the whole class, plenty of display areas

From the point of view of the reader, there are areas:

- **For selecting reading material:** a class library area, reference shelves, discussion areas, book displays
- **For reading:** open floor space, corrals, in plan two: withdrawal room, comfortable, well-lit spaces for individual and shared reading
- **For sharing reading:** follow up productions: e.g. posters, using bookmaking materials, papers, art materials; display boards, walls, tables, class reading, retelling, storytelling, reviewing, readers' theatre, drama: open floor area.

The layouts lend themselves to multiple activities happening concurrently. The classroom is, in fact, a workshop area where I expect that children will be:

- working at their own pace
- working at their own level
- working at their own interest
- working at their own activity

The classroom layout must cater for this individual difference by providing a wide variety of work areas.

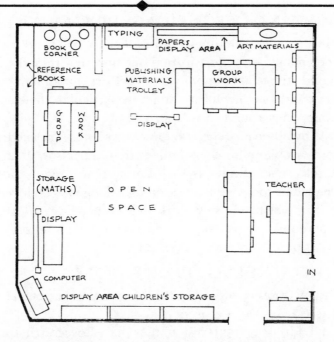

Classroom layout: plan one

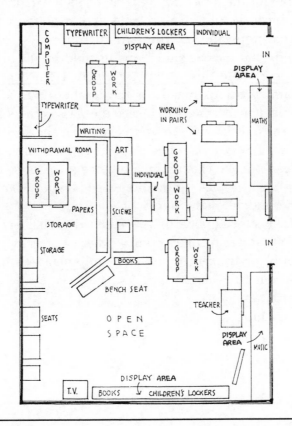

Classroom layout: plan two

MAKING THE CLASSROOM ATTRACTIVE

Most people, including children, like to look good and they spend time and money and effort in making sure that they do. Most people also spend time and money and effort in making sure they have surroundings they like to be in: in particular, their homes and gardens where they spend the most time.

Why? Because people are stimulated, relaxed, interested, and comfortable in an environment that appeals to them. They feel good. Surely this attitude towards our environment must extend to the classroom too. If the classroom looks good, children feel good in it. If they feel good, they work well. When the children know that it is 'our room', they are happy to spend time and effort on its appearance — pride of ownership is important.

ORGANISING THE ROOM

Organisation is important too. To maintain a clean and attractive room it is essential to be organised.

Children lose interest if they have to scratch through cupboards containing years of accumulated magazines, old tins and jars, the previous teacher's unwanted cardboard signs and the crepe paper rolls, looking for the bookbinding tape for their exciting new book they have just finished. Piles of unrelated and forgotten debris in corners and on benchtops are far from stimulating.

And what message am I giving children if I leave it there? Maybe, 'I do not value this workplace where I am expecting you to learn.'

I am conscious that I, as the teacher, must demonstrate the care and maintenance needed to keep the classroom looking good. It actually took me a little while to appreciate that the saying 'Why me?' should actually be 'Why *not* me?', especially in reference to who was going to clean out the class guinea pig's cage, or prise the thumb tacks out of the wall, or pick up the over-ripe banana which had been dropped in the middle of the doorway.

Make sure cupboards are labelled accurately with a list of their contents and that children know where materials are stored. Don't keep rubbish, or broken or unused equipment: it's cluttering. Two good classroom rules are:
- everything works
- everything has a place

3
PROVIDING
RESOURCES

Just about anything can be considered a resource for the classroom. I look at everything with a view to possible uses, and then I put it away (in an organised fashion) against the day it will come in handy.

What do children need in their learning environment?

WRITING NEEDS
PLANNING AND DRAFTING WRITING
While they are planning and drafting, children need:
- lots of reference materials of all sorts for their pre-writing planning; ideas from everywhere as catalysts for stimulating writing
- dictionaries, and not a class set of identical dictionaries, but a class set of many different dictionaries
- a draft book for each child to be used for *all* drafts of writing. Using a book gives value to the writing drafts; using old computer paper stapled together does not.

DRAFT BOOKS
Children must be able to look back over their drafts to see what they need to do now, basing their plans on what they have already done. Drafts done on scraps of paper, 'rough' copies, become lost, torn, discarded. Eventually, children don't know what they have done in the past, so how can they plan for the future?

The **teacher** must be able to look back over the drafts to see what is needed to program for each child now, based on what she/he perceives as developmental needs. The child's draft book is an important part of the assessment profile for each child.

The **parents** must be able to look back over the drafts to see how their child's written language has developed over a period. A useful letter to staple into the writer's draft book is this:

Dear Parents,

These books contain your child's own words, sentences and stories for 199-. The children have worked very hard in these books.

It doesn't matter if the words, etc. aren't right. Remember that these books represent first attempts to get thoughts down on paper! The finished product is the published book.

Encourage and praise all attempts your child makes to read and write, just as you encouraged his/her early attempts to speak.

Ask your child to tell you about the writing. Sometimes he/she will not remember what the story was about (some of these stories were written 10 months ago). Ask to be told about the pictures. Then you can reply, 'That's what it says, doesn't it. I am riding my bike!'

Enjoy the writing, as we have!

P/1/2 Teachers

Letter to parents to accompany draft books

Even if parents are very supportive of this approach to learning, this letter may still reassure.

DRAFT BOOK ESSENTIALS

Children put a *Have a Go* sheet on the back inside cover of their draft books — spelling is visual, and if children see their attempts at spelling a word they may recognise an error, and be likely to write the word correctly at their next attempt.

NAME: _____ HAVE A GO !!!		
First try	Second try	Correct word

Have a go sheet

I also work with children to produce editing checkpoints for them to keep in their draft books as a guide for their personal editing of their writing. The 'S-factor' was a very successful editing list developed by a Year 3/4 group to help them when they were editing their drafts. Other year levels used them too.

BEFORE anyone else reads your story

CONSIDER THE S-FACTOR

Does your story make SENSE?

Is the STRUCTURE sound?

How is the SPELLING?

* NOW have someone else read your story.

S-factor sheet

This sheet was pasted into the front of their draft books as a ready reference for them.

Other groups might produce more complex lists.

PERSONAL EDITING CHECKLIST

My Ideas:
Does my title tell you about my main idea?
Will my idea interest a reader?
Can I improve my ideas?

My Organisation:
Is my opening interesting for my reader?
Is there a good sequence of events?
Will my reader understand my ideas?
Can I improve my ending?

My Language:
Is my language suitable for my reader?
Is my language suitable for the story?
Have I used words that are not important to the story?
Is my language interesting?
Can I improve or change any words I have used?

My Mechanics:
Have I checked my spelling
                  punctuation
                  apostrophes
                  dialogue
                  sentences
                  paragraphs
Have I presented this piece of writing neatly and attractively?

Year 8 editing checklist

OTHER WRITER'S ESSENTIALS

It is useful to have editing 'reminder' lists posted about the room too. In fact, the room will probably be covered with writing of all kinds. In my classroom the walls, the furniture and all available surfaces are covered with writing: lists, cartoons, messages, statements, stories, scripts, predictions, surveys, word maps, summaries, brainstorms, drafts, instructions, reports, diaries, definitions, programs, invitations, songs, recipes, conclusions, data collections, records, notes, text passages, reviews, references, verse, journals, descriptions, resolutions, reminders, rules.

The collection builds up over time. By the end of the year, there is no empty space in the room at all. Writing even hangs from the ceiling. You can hardly see out the windows. The room contains more Blu Tack than the rest of the school combined.

In this classroom you can usually count on being in trouble with the school cleaner. They hate crawling through it all, trailing their vacuum cleaners in the hope of seeing a little vacant space to actually clean. I let them know at the very beginning of the year why the room needs to be like this, that everything in it is there because the whole room is a resource for the children's learning, and everything has a part to play in that learning.

The writing is clean, neat, well-presented and clearly readable; it is functional and attractive. It is *not* yellowing at the edges, faded to the point of illegibility, tattered, hanging in curling pieces, irrelevant to the learning.

Most of the writing is done by the children; if it is written by me it can be clearly seen to relate to the children's learning needs. It is their resource. Every day:

- one child at least will refer to a vocabulary list on the back wall for a word needed in a piece of writing
- a group of children will consult a set of instructions they need to follow to complete their project
- the whole class will add to a topic word list. They may work with a list to classify their understandings about a topic by grouping words under headings, or they may draft statements from lists to clarify their ideas about a topic.

PUBLISHING WRITING

Use whatever can be begged, borrowed or bought, including, if you can:

- manual typewriters, big and small print
- electric typewriters, big and small print
- computers and printers
- book binding machine, book bindings

- guillotine
- clear adhesive plastic for book covering
- papers of all sorts, including exotic papers
- coloured tapes
- staplers
- hole punchers
- writing and drawing materials of all kinds
- blank big books, for class stories.

Having everything stored appropriately, with easy access, well-labelled with directions for use, makes for efficient running of the classroom workshop.

READING NEEDS

For reading, children need the widest range of reading material obtainable. In my classroom, **books are everywhere**. They cover every flat surface. I have never had a book corner that was adequate.

- The children can choose from magazines, newspapers, journals.
- We subscribe to children's book clubs such as Eyespy, Puffinalia, Geo, Lucky, Comet, Challenge, Explore.
- We collect specialist and hobby magazines such as *Royalauto*, *Police News*, *Stamp News*, *Good Weekend*. There is excitement when the latest issue of a favourite magazine arrives.
- The children and I bulk-borrow from the school library.
- We borrow from local libraries.
- We read from reading schemes.
- The children have bring-and-borrow sessions, using their own books.
- They read books written by class members.
- They read my books.
- They read junk mail and pamphlets, trade journals, manuals, how to's, travel guides.
- I keep a set of encyclopedias in the room, along with atlases, dictionaries, thesauruses, and other reference books.

A lot of the reading materials are there because of children's interests, hobbies, and classroom topics. When you are collecting reading materials:

- observe what each child likes to read
- talk to them about their reading
- keep their reading interests in mind when you are looking at reading materials
- beg, borrow or buy reading materials **with particular children in mind**
- remember the classroom topic being studied at the time, and collect materials that give information about that topic.

WHAT NOW?

Of course, it is not enough to simply bring together the resources, the place and the time and set the children down expecting that learning will occur. These three things simply set the scene by creating a likely learning environment. Learning and teaching can now begin.

PART TWO

MAKING LEARNING EASIER
FOR LEARNERS

4

INTEGRATING THE CONDITIONS OF LEARNING

◆

As well as planning and structuring the classroom environment, the teacher has the task of planning and implementing program topics to stimulate learning. What topics will be able to sustain all the conditions for learning? What needs to be considered when planning those topics?

TOPIC PLANNING CONSIDERATIONS

1 KNOW THE CHILDREN

The first thing to know is the children in the classroom. Then you will know what topic will engage their attention, what topic will have enough variety of content so that there will be something for everyone contained in it, something to actively involve all. Will the topic cater for the children's experiences and interests, and build upon them, make links with their learning from their past and into their future? What have children learnt in other places? Will they have the opportunity to pursue and express their ideas? Can the topic cater for the diversity of skills and aptitudes in the group, and foster the development of these?

2 OVERVIEW THE WHOLE TOPIC

I begin developing a unit of work by ignoring traditional subject barriers. Integrating all subject areas is an ideal way to ensure that all conditions for learning will be present, and I can review and document the subjects that are covered by the topic while it is underway.

In the beginning, I look at the whole topic, its possible content, the possible learning processes that can be introduced, practised, and mastered by the children during the time the topic is underway.

3 INVOLVE THE CHILDREN
Give the children responsibility for decisions about the content of the topic and the planning of activities. Let them share the responsibility for implementing the topic activities and performing the tasks.

4 BUILD IN CO-OPERATION
Along the way, children will probably plan to work individually, in groups, and with all their classmates. As teacher, I also plan activities that will develop the social skills of co-operation and communication that are important for achievement of tasks. I look for opportunities during the course of the topic where children need to share responsibility in order to achieve goals.

5 ALLOW PLENTY OF TIME
Give children plenty of time and opportunity to investigate a topic, to explore their understandings of it and evaluate their findings. They need to be able to reflect on their work, testing new theories they might now have against their previous ideas and the ideas of others in the room. When does a topic finish? For some children, the topic might be a trigger for a lifetime interest, and therefore NEVER finish!

STEPS TO TOPIC DEVELOPMENT
I find that integrated topic planning and programming is very complex.

1   Initially, I must explore the topic myself.
    a I establish my own understanding of its content.
    b I look at my purposes for the topic in terms of the learning experiences it will offer the children, and the reasons for wanting the children to have those experiences.
    c I decide on a focus that will establish a starting point and stimulate initial discussion and exploration of the topic by the children. The focus might be simple, a class discussion about the topic, or something fairly dramatic, such as an experiment or an excursion.
2   As the work gets underway, the children's understandings will direct the topic.
    a The children will begin to make decisions and act upon them; their experiences and interests brought to the work will influence directions it takes.
    b Their understandings of the topic will develop and new perceptions of it will alter the sequence of it.
3   My role will change.
    a One constant part of my role will be that I will continue to

guide, defining the parameters of the topic, keeping the topic in focus to help the children in their activity.

b I must consistently observe and listen, so that I will be aware of needs as they appear, 'striking while the iron is hot', guiding children's strategies and helping them develop new ones as they are needed.

c I must provide material resources as they are required.

d I must focus on changes in direction, ensuring that children are aware that these have occurred.

e And all the time I will be observing and assessing children's progress, the processes they are using and the understandings about the topic they are developing.

CASE STUDY: AN INVESTIGATION OF FAIRYTALES

One integrated learning topic I undertook a few years ago was with a Year 3/4 composite class. The topic was fairytales, and the children remained motivated and involved throughout.

1 INITIAL TEACHER PLANNING

WHAT IS A FAIRYTALE?

I needed to be very clear in my own mind about fairytales: what exactly were they, what specific characteristics did they have? I collected as many fairytales as I could, read them, and formed my own opinion of the characteristics of fairytales. I read other peoples' opinions, in journals and literature studies, and I discussed with my colleagues. I jotted down ideas and information. I began to classify my collection.

WHAT WERE MY AIMS AND OBJECTIVES FOR THIS TOPIC?

1   I had observed that a number of children in the class were only using a personal narrative style in their own writing, for example, they were writing diary type stories. They were not consciously using other styles of book language and their writing reflected this.

I wanted to saturate them with another style, with the intention of giving them another formula to use in their writing. I wanted to stimulate their ideas for their writing, and to give them the support they might need to try another writing form.

2   Children's reading choices were not as wide-ranging as they could be, particularly among the large group of boys in the class. To put it bluntly, if it wasn't about sport, the boys weren't reading it.

I wanted to develop positive attitudes towards other genres, encouraging children to try those outside their normal range of choice.

Wensday 28 Feb   My Birthday   Gordon

Last year   on   the 11th of December. I had
my birthday I got two models One from Lukas,
and I got another from Rohan. Then we went
to the park and we palyed baseball. My
team won. Then we went back to my my house
and I opened my presants. Igot sink the fleet
from Robet and a set of aeroplanes from
Stuart. and a basketball from Robin.

The   End

My birthday: an example of a 'diary' story

I wanted to give children an opportunity to explore beyond the concerns of their immediate experience, and to begin to look at fictional worlds.

3 Quite a number of children in the class were beginning to struggle with the organisation of their stories, working with plot development and sequence, thinking about setting and characterisation. Some were beginning to develop a personal style, and they were trying to add description and mood and emotion to their stories. Others were approximating stories and styles with which they were familiar.

I wanted to give the children some very clear demonstrations of story, and fairytales would illustrate very simply the essential components of story: setting, characterisation, and plot development. Fairytales were also rich in emotive language and description.

I wanted children to make connections between one book and another, developing an understanding of the conventions of story, using fairytales as the example.

4 The class had not looked at a particular genre before. Their previous topics had included an author study (Robin Klein), a character study (Ralph, a speed-crazy mouse constantly in search of excitement, in books by Beverley Cleary), and reading and writing some poetry forms including limericks and haiku.

I wanted children to study a traditional story type, and become familiar with its characteristics. I wanted them to know that the fairytale is part of our culture, and should therefore be part of our common knowledge.

WHAT SPECIFIC SKILLS DID I WANT CHILDREN TO DEVELOP?

I planned to demonstrate a number of skills, and then give the children the opportunity to experience and experiment with these using the topic content.

1 *How to plan and write a summary.* This skill would be useful to them when writing book reviews, in discussions and in response to books, films, etc., and when reading books to use other authors' ideas for their own writing.

2 *How to write scripts and dialogue,* from simple readers theatre presentations, 'interviews' with book characters, for example, interviewing the giant, Jack's mother and Jack to hear the story from different perspectives, to 'hypothetical' dramas, for example, Sleeping Beauty sleeps longer than planned and she wakes up in the year 2050 — what did she wake up to, how did she cope, what did the rest of her court do? I wanted children to have the experience of planning, scripting and staging a full play as well.

3 *To build fairytale (and hence story) vocabulary lists* on wall charts that children could use as reference for their own writing.

4 *To write a class story* based on a fairytale text so that children could become aware that other people's stories could be used as a source for their own stories.

5 *To work in co-operative groups,* building up interdependent relationships within the class by working together on common tasks.

WHAT WILL BE THE INITIAL FOCUS FOR THE TOPIC?

To begin the topic, I decided to draw upon children's experience with fairytales. I would read them a very traditional version of a fairytale they would probably all know well, and encourage them to discuss and share their experiences of the fairytale: where they first heard it, who told them, could they remember their initial reactions to the story, what about the story caused this reaction, what was their response now, what had caused the difference, did they know the story by heart, what type of story was this?

By encouraging the children to share their past experiences and express their present views about fairytales, I was drawing them into the topic, giving them a jumping-off point for their own further exploration.

2. THE TOPIC DEVELOPS

TOPIC OUTLINE

The next step was to plan a sequence of activities over a five-week period to achieve my objectives. Of course, I expected that the children would develop their own objectives and activities for the topic as we got underway with it, so my plan was very skeletal. I wanted the children to flesh it out with their experiences, understandings, interests and skills as they began their own inquiries into the topic.

My initial 'plan', shown opposite, included the content, skills, focuses and activities that I felt could be included in such a unit. This was drawn from my own understandings of fairytales, my aims for the topic, the specific skills I wanted to develop, and the input from the children.

DETAILED TOPIC SEQUENCE

This is what happened.

Each week began with a focus that would provide starting points for investigating the topic. Skills were demonstrated, and tasks related to the topic that would allow practice of these skills were developed by the children and myself.

Week one

Focus one: To find out what the children know about fairytales.

Activity: I read the class 'Hansel and Gretel' by the Brothers Grimm, illustrated by Anthony Browne. The story was discussed, using the discussion starters from the initial teacher plan.

- What type of story is this?
  When the answer 'fairytale' came up, words and phrases that described what the children knew of fairytales were written on a wall chart.
  Children were already familiar with story-writing terminology — character, setting and plot, so these words were used as headings on the wall chart.

Review: It was clear that at this stage children had a wide range of specific understandings about fairytales. The words and phrases they were using belonged to specific stories. They were not making generalisations about fairytales as a genre. For example, 'fairies' were listed as characters in fairytales, yet very few fairytales actually have fairies as characters.

Focus two: To further develop children's understanding of fairytales, leading to an ability to make generalisations.

* FIRST SESSION — what characters do you find in fairytales?
BRAINSTORM — where do fairytales happen?
what happens in fairytales?

establish a fairytale

ORAL — 'interview' fairytale character — eg B. Briggs fairy godmother

fairytale reading centre

SHORT PLAYS/ROLE PLAYS — some commercial — oral retelling — texts

What do children know?

WANT LIST: Books and stories that are not definitely fts

EXPLORATION OF PLOT — writing summaries — precis writing

Modelled writing → writing moves by tr

class wall frieze of fairytales

RESEARCH — groups of 3 — significance in legends magic

EXTENDING READING INTERESTS — moving away from the ½ Fr. — Enid B. & the ½ Fr.

"CRACKED" Tale eg Craig & the Mean Hawk

WALL STORY — whole group fairytale — exploring the genre in non-threatening situation

TR READS → modelling fairytales good reading daily practice

MATHS — graphs ← shoe sizes (Sw + Ha ?D) — 7x table — 3x Table — estimate beans in jar — strategies for estimation

ART — make puppets, costumes, masks — fairytale panorama

SCIENCE — growing beans — needs

EXPOSURE TO RANGE OF AUTHOR STORY TYPES

SHARED WRITING

FAIRYTALES — focus: the genre

compare — plots — episodes — settings

WHOLE CLASS

ACTIVITY — ORAL — informal debate — The Best 3 wishes — state why, support your opinion

TYPES OF ANIMALS IN FAIRYTALES — why wolves? RESEARCH

LAST SESSION: what do children know? Now

WALL WORD LISTS — word building — whole group

INDIVIDUAL WORKING — Chris's own writing — explore genre — when confident to do so — evaluation + review conference

SPELLING — from wordlist → HEAVY DUTY WORDS for GENRE STUDY — own writing — group work — individually checked

what is a fairytale? do fairytales follow a pattern? is there fairytale language? are there modern fairytales?

→ WALL CHART — STARWARS? — STARWARS? → WALL CHART

*Fairytales: criteria — animals? — magic? — royalty?

RESEARCH — there dwarfs were...

CONFERENCES — individual — group + troubleshooting conference — sharing — celebrating

PUBLISH
GROUP STORY WRITING — using spelling words — exploring genre in non-threatening situation

what is a changeling? — make a family tree for a ROYAL FAMILY

OPINION POLLS — who is the most EVIL character? — bravest hero? why? — most beautiful heroine? — record votes + reasons

MUSIC — CHANTS — once upon a time — nursery rhyme — whole group innovations

tallest because... — measure — daily, diag, record growth → MATHS

art water? light? soil?

DALE GORDON
Year 3/4 CLASS
INTEGRATED LEARNING UNIT 1988
LITERATURE BASED, CO-OPERATIVE LEARNING TECHNIQUES.

Five-week outline: Fairytales

WHAT CHARACTERS DO YOU FIND IN FAIRYTALES? (Characters)

*fairies   *dwarfs
*princesses   *giants
*kings *queen *stepmothers
*dragons

WHERE DO FAIRYTALES HAPPEN? (Setting)

*anywhere   *castles and poor cottages
*a long time ago   *woods

WHAT HAPPENS IN FAIRYTALES (Plot)

*magic spells, someone gets poisoned
*the prince saves the princess
*the stepmother is cruel to the children
*they get rich

Fairytales wall chart

Activity one: I read another fairytale, reading as many versions of this tale as possible, for example, 'Jack and the Beanstalk': a traditional version; a very old version; one by Roald Dahl, in *Revolting Rhymes*; 'Jack and the Tinstalk', by Michael Rosen in *Hairy Tales and Nursery Crimes*; and *Jim and the Beanstalk* by Raymond Briggs.

We discussed what changed, and what hadn't changed in these variations. Were they all still fairytales? Why?

Activity two: The children were encouraged to 'interview' the characters from the different versions, to highlight the differences and the similarities of each version

Review: This session provoked a great deal of class discussion. Children began to look for other fairytales with more than one version. Some children began a register, to record the number of versions of particular fairytales.

The children decided to set up a 'fairytale corner'. A stockpile of fairytale books from the library, their own collections, and my collection began to accumulate, and this became a very popular spot during silent reading times.

By the end of week one, children were becoming intrigued by fairytales. Even those 'heavies' who had considered the topic a little 'immature' at first were beginning to enjoy the activities.

The topic was beginning to be shaped by the children. They wanted to write plays from fairytales, they were writing lists grouping fairytales by title and character, and had started a vocabulary list on a wall chart.

Week two

Focus one: To highlight the particular features of fairytales again.

34

Over the next few weeks I planned to look at fairytales by different authors to find out what could be different and what stayed the same in fairytales, even if authors had different approaches, styles, language, plot, settings and characters.

Activity: Each day of week two, I read fairytales by the Brothers Grimm. We discussed what characteristics made them fairytales, and what characterised fairytales by the Brothers Grimm. Listening to these tales became the favourite class activity.

Focus two: Summary writing.

Once again, we could draw out the essential characteristics of fairytales as we focused on the key elements of them for our summary writing.

I first needed to ensure that all children understood what a summary was, so some time was spent defining summary, looking at examples in magazines, book blurbs, newspapers, etc. We looked at the purposes for summary writing generally, and established a purpose for the activity.

Activity: Everyone would write a summary of their favourite fairytale and the summaries would then be displayed as a wall frieze to use as a 'ready reference' of known fairytales.

I demonstrated writing a summary, accepting editing comment from the children as I wrote. I chose to summarise a traditional version of 'Jack and the Beanstalk' because the tale was very well known by all the children and they would therefore be able to see that I was drawing the key elements from the tale in my summary.

Jack and his mother were very poor.
They sold their cow for 5 beans.
The beans grew into a giant beanstalk.
Jack climbed to its top.
A giant lived there.
Jack stole his money, his magic hen and his magic harp.
He killed the giant and chopped down the beanstalk.
He and his mother were rich.

Using the same process, children produced their own summaries, and illustrated them for public display as a wall frieze.

Review: By the end of week two, children had initiated many of the directions the topic was taking.

- Other class wall lists were being pasted up as well as the vocabulary list, titles of fairytales, list of phrases used in fairytales.
- Children were using various criteria to classify the fairytale book collection, by authors, titles, settings, etc. As they ordered and classified their information, their understanding of the characteristics of fairytales continued to grow.

- A few children had begun to write their own fairytales or were paraphrasing published ones as their familiarity with the form brought confidence.
- The topic had moved into other 'subject' areas. A group of children had begun to experiment with growing beans. They had planted a number of beans, each bean under a different set of conditions in order to establish what conditions would be required to grow the largest plant. The progress of the beans was being graphed daily.

  Who anticipated this development and made sure that the materials for this experiment were available? Providing resources is **always** part of the teacher's role.
- Several groups of children were making dioramas of their favourite fairytale.
- Two groups were producing fairytale plays, and were involved in writing the scripts and making props, costumes, and masks for their productions.
- Children were raiding libraries, other classrooms, their friends and family members in their search for fairytales.

Week three

Focus one: To further develop children's understanding of fairytales, leading to an ability to make generalisations.

Activity one: I continued to read fairytales in week three, concentrating in particular on tales by Charles Perrault, and 'fractured' fairytales by Michael Rosen, Fiona French and Roald Dahl.

Children's understandings of fairytales were challenged, especially by the 'fractured' fairytales.

Activity two: In order to check their understanding that even 'fractured' fairytales were fairytales, the children were encouraged to write a class story, their own 'fractured' fairytale. They chose to write after the style of Michael Rosen, and based the story on 'Jack and the Beanstalk'. It was eventually titled 'Craig and the Mean Hawk'. All children had the opportunity to participate in this writing, and those who felt uncertain about their fairytale writing skills could practise writing one within the security of a large group.

Focus two: To increase personal writing vocabulary, especially of words that would be useful to children writing their own fairytales.

Activity: The children chose a class spelling list of thirty-two words from the wall chart lists of fairytale vocabulary.

The class was divided into groups, which were chosen to be as equal as possible, and each group had to plan and demonstrate strategies to ensure that group members learned the chosen words. The groups planned to use the words to write group fairytales in following weeks, so they had purpose in learning the words for that activity.

I had several teacher's purposes. I wanted the children to focus on the words that are part of fairytale language. I was keen as well to give them as many reasons as possible for working together in small groups. And this was a good opportunity for me to observe the strategies children used for learning to spell. I could take note of those children who would need to have more attention in the future.

fairy	another	witch	dungeon
market	poison	stepmother	message
once	prince	spell	crown
happily	princess	magic	slipper
forest	dragon	wishes	knight
upon	fierce	mountain	dreams
after	strange	sword	thunder
evil	wizard	cast	midnight

Fairytales word list

Review: By the end of this third week, spin-offs from the topic included the following:

- Children were reading fairytales during silent reading time, and for home reading. Bookings were taken for popular stories. Children from other classes were coming into the classroom to:
    read from our collection
    bring us more fairytales
    borrow from the fairytale corner
    be an audience for performances of fairytale drama productions.
- An opinion poll was conducted by one group to find out which characters from fairytales were considered to be:
    the most evil
    the most beautiful
    the most popular
- A fairytale definition list had been established:
    What was the exact meaning of changeling?
    What was the difference between goblin, dwarf, elf, troll?
- A group of children were researching the significance of the number three in fairytales, and its place in mythology and legends.
- Another group were investigating wolves, to find out why they had a bad reputation in fairytales.
- Four children were graphing the most popular wishes to find out which three were the class favourites.
- The beans continued to grow, and their progress was charted on the graph. 'Leftover' beans were put in a jar. I asked the children to write a report on how they would go about estimating the number of beans in the jar: a 'strike while the iron is hot' teacher strategy.

- Fourteen children (out of twenty-one) were writing their own fairytales, and there was plenty of sharing and conferences as their stories began to take shape.

Very little of this activity had been generated by me; the class had almost completely taken control of the topic. I did call regular daily meetings with the whole class in order to familiarise everyone with the activities that were happening, to co-ordinate, plan and timetable (especially the drama performances), to seek advice, and to collect resources.

Week four
Focus one: To continue to develop children's understanding of fairytales, leading to an ability to make generalisations.
Activity: During week four I read fairytales by Hans Christian Anderson every day.

Focus two: Has everyone learnt the spelling words: are the words now part of each child's spelling repertoire? Which groups have been successful in teaching all their members to spell the words?
Activity: A spelling tournament was held to see how well groups had learnt the fairytale vocabulary words. The learning strategies each group used to ensure all their members learned the words were discussed and shared with the whole class.

Focus three: Can all children now make generalisations about the fairytale genre?
Activity: Groups were asked to write a fairytale that used all spelling words.
Review: By the end of this week, some children were publishing individual fairytales and, as well, the group stories were well underway. Conference time revealed that most children could now make generalisations about fairytales. They could give reasoned arguments, criticisms and suggestions to support their opinions when discussing the writing of the genre. They could say which stories were *not* fairytales.

The drama performances, interviews, opinion polls, and research continued through this week, but we were moving towards a finale in week five.

Week five
Focus: Review, what do we know *now* about fairytales?
Activity one: This week I read fairytales that were uncommon, or non-traditional, as well as reading children's own published fairytales and the group stories, now published in an anthology, and a big favourite for borrowing during silent reading time.

Activity two: We once again brainstormed what children knew about fairytales, this time attempting to draw generalisations using the wall lists of specific data that had been collected and the children's personal understanding.

Children now clearly made generalisations about the fairytale genre. Their ideas about characters, setting and plot had moved from specific understandings of single stories to broad statements. Some class statements were made:

'Fairytale characters are either good or bad.'

'Generally, the bad are ugly, and the good are handsome.'

'Fairytales happen somewhere that is not true, in another world.'

'The goodies win, the baddies lose.'

'At the end of the story, they live happily ever after.'

Activity three: The final planned session of this topic was to watch a video of the film *Star Wars*. Was this a fairytale? There was little debate: the characters, setting and plot clearly matched the children's understanding of fairytale genre.

Review: The end of week five marked the end of the topic.

- Some children were still deeply involved, and they continued their study of fairytales for some time further.
- Some children were beginning to extend their interests to other related literature, such as fantasy, folk tales, myths and legends, and science fiction. They were using their understanding of fairytales for investigations of their own. This was a clear move for some away from their previous reading and writing interests.
- For some children, this was the first time they had become aware that stories could actually be classified into types according to specific characteristics. The characteristics of language, form, character, setting, and plot peculiar to particular genres, in this case fairytales, was highlighted for them.
- Other children had written a story that was not a personal narrative for the first time. The benefits of shared writing sessions, and class and group story writing, in providing opportunities to support learning were clear.
- The class had become more cohesive as a group. They now had common experiences and common knowledge to unite them, as well as understandings about the behaviours that are needed to make group work a success.
- Most class members had participated in a drama activity, performing some of the tasks that are part of that process.

MEETING THE CONDITIONS OF LEARNING

Looking back to my objectives for the topic, I could see clearly that they all had been met. One of the last parts of my teacher's role, to record my assessment of children's learning during the topic, was easy. In what direction should the next topic lead these children? Maybe to look at factual texts, to develop concepts of the differences in text types.

This topic had engaged all children in a series of learning tasks for five weeks. Had the conditions for learning been operating during that period? Yes.

- Very obviously, the children had taken responsibility for their learning activities with minimum direction from me after the first initial scene setting.
- They had decided what they would learn about the topic, following their own interests and becoming involved in those aspects of the topic. There were many examples of this: the group of children who experimented with differences in growth rates of beans by varying growing conditions, others who made dioramas, and struggled with materials and perspectives, still others who classified and documented information about fairytales.
- They were all expected to learn and to share what they had learnt with the whole group at the daily meetings and in group activities.
- They were given the time, and resources with which to learn; this was part of my role.
- They had opportunities to practise, sometimes in a directed activity such as the summary writing, sometimes in sheltering and non-threatening activities such as whole class and group story writing.
- They had many demonstrations of what they were expected to learn; fairytales were read to them every day, the classroom was full of fairytale language, and other children and I were working all around them.
- There was immediate response to their activity: at the daily meetings, during conferences. Stories written by the children were always read, opinions and criticisms were always offered. Because most children were working independently at any one time my time was available for discussion and advice to individuals who needed it, at the time they needed it.

The advantages of this type of programming were very clear.

5

PROVIDING REAL REASONS TO LEARN

◆

Successful learning requires that learners have at least one good reason for that learning. Hopefully, they have more than one.

Therefore, I must program to give children realistic tasks where they can see what's in it for them, where the tasks will fulfil their learning needs and wants, and give them good reasons to learn.

I must therefore have clear reasons of my own for setting learning tasks: there need to be good reasons for choosing what is to be taught too. Children readily pick up which tasks are just 'busy' work, with no purpose at all. I need to demonstrate to them that learning is always for a good reason by making sure that the tasks they are asked to perform in my classroom do have a purpose.

Back in the 'golden olden' days, teachers planned most programs to promote children's learning of content. For example, spelling words were chosen and learned by rote learning methods on Monday to Thursday, then on Friday came the 'dictation test', to see what the children had 'learnt' during the week. The facts, in this case the spelling of the words, are only the surface layer of the content, of course; these days we want children to probe deeper, look behind the facts, and under and beside, and begin to investigate the understandings and the concepts on which the facts are based.

The learning of content, while important, is not enough. As well, we want children to develop learning skills and processes they can use to further investigate facts. We want them to be learners who know how to go about finding the facts they want. And we want the learning of these skills and processes to become some of the reasons the children have for learning.

We must therefore set overriding aims and objectives for our programs which ensure that the learning has this depth, and will therefore be more likely to meet children's present and future reasons for learning. Furthermore, we should be very sure that the children are aware of these aims and objectives too, and know why they are there.

PROGRAM AIMS AND OBJECTIVES

1 INFORMATION-GATHERING SKILLS

Children must be given the opportunity to use and develop information-gathering skills that will give them independence and flexibility in their approach to their learning, when it really matters.

Programs must allow children to:

observe
share information
analyse
infer
interpret
classify
explore
investigate
compare and contrast
plan
collect
explain
discuss
identify
construct
list
categorise
research
evaluate outcomes by predicting
generalising
reflecting
recording
assessing
using
presenting
discussing

2 LITERACY AND NUMERACY SKILLS

I want children to know that they really do need to develop proficient skills in:

reading

writing

speaking

listening

spelling

computing, etc.

so that they can use these skills in a wide variety of contexts and for many different purposes.

3 SOCIAL AND COMMUNICATION SKILLS

I want children to know that working with others is an expectation of our society. Therefore, my programming must allow children time to work with others co-operatively, practising social skills that will foster interdependence.

4 LATERAL THINKING SKILLS

I want children to know that learning is interrelated. Subjects such as mathematics and the study of society are not isolated entities, they are part of a whole. Let children think about what subjects are interrelated when they go on a shopping trip to the local supermarket with their parents!

Programs should reflect this by presenting integrated work units that cut across traditional and artificial subject barriers.

In my classroom I have further overriding aims and objectives for the learning programs the children and I develop

1 FLEXIBLE

I want children to understand that the program in the classroom will be flexible, and will meet the needs and purposes of each participating individual and cater for their

creativity

interest

curiosity

learning capacity

2 INFORMATIVE

I want the program to give information about the children and their learning, to guide future programming for each child. I want each child to know that I am interested in finding out about their learning and that they need to monitor their learning and make decisions about it too. I want them to be active, not passive learners!

PROGRAMMING TO ACHIEVE THESE PURPOSES

A program that aimed to achieve these general purposes, plus other specific objectives, was a language workshop for a Year 6 group. The workshop was started at the beginning of the school year after the long summer vacation. It was called 'Summertime' and it began on day one. My aims were:

1 To gain initial information about the language development of individual children in the group.

2 To use that information to see where programming should focus for the term, and the year. Therefore, the workshop was designed to demonstrate children's language competence in a large number of areas.

SUMMERTIME WORKSHOP: YEAR 6
EXPECTATIONS

---

1 During the next four weeks you are expected to produce a folio of work under this title.

2 The folio should include a title page, general introduction, all writing drafts as well as editing sheets and final written presentations. Presentation of your folio is important.

3 Drafts are to be conferenced by your editor and/or me weekly. Use the editing sheet in your folio for this purpose.

4 Work in the folio will come from the following sources:
   a class and group work on the topic, 'Summertime'
   b one piece of independent writing
   c one book review, format to be discussed in class
   d two pieces of writing chosen from titles decided by the class.

The class discussed and then listed titles from which they would select two to write on for section 4d of their folios.

CLASS TITLES: choose two
- Summertime, and the living is easy
- My favourite summer treat, and how to make it
- New year's resolutions
- Beating the holiday blues: a cure for boredom
- The best day of the whole holiday
- The greatest danger of summer is...

The editing sheet was distributed and explained. Children chose another class member as their editor, someone with whom they felt they could work effectively, and the workshop began. The role of editor was discussed, and children wrote a list of possible duties for editors, and displayed the list as a wall chart'for reference.

WORKSHOP DIARY SHEET	NAME: _____	
Title	Date/comment	Name
Presentation of folio:		

Workshop diary sheet

Exactly what could I find out about the children from this workshop? The first two expectations, covering the production of the folio, would allow me to observe information-gathering skills such as:

organising
planning
collecting
collating
presenting
reporting
time management

The third expectation, the editing tasks, would allow me to observe further information-gathering skills such as:

observing
sharing
analysing
interpreting
identifying
explaining
discussing

evaluating
reflecting
and social skills such as:
sharing
working with others
being interdependent
accepting and giving constructive criticism

The fourth expectation, which set out the tasks to be completed, would give me the opportunity to observe many aspects of children's literacy skills, as well as their information-gathering skills.

FINDING OUT ABOUT LITERACY SKILLS

LOOKING AT CHILDREN'S INDEPENDENT WRITING

By asking the children to produce a piece of writing independently, I hoped to be able to achieve the following objectives:

1 To assess children's individual development as writers, looking at their topic ideas, sources of these ideas, their interests and influence.

2 I wanted to look at their language usage, particularly story development and story sequencing. What types of stories were they comfortable writing, and what types would they need further experience with in the future?

3 I wanted to look at how they structured language, particularly sentence structure and paragraphing.

4 I wanted to look at their language usage, particularly dialogue, apostrophes, tenses, etc.

5 I wanted to observe their spelling, and the strategies they used.

6 I wanted to look at their drafting and production techniques, to observe their capacity and willingness to act upon editorial opinion, and to assess their editorial skills.

LOOKING AT CHILDREN'S BOOK REVIEWS

This writing of the book reviews was given a special purpose by the children. They decided that all reviews would be published in a class reference book, which they named 'Great Reading for Year 6 Readers'.

My objectives for the book reviews were as follows:

1 To assess children's experience and competence to read and retell their reading.

2 To assess their capacity to express a personal opinion.

3 To ascertain children's reading interests.

4 To observe children working together to produce one product, a class book of their book reviews, to ascertain their capacity to work together as a group.

DEMONSTRATING THE PROCESS

I needed to show the children how to write a book review, as this was a new skill for this class. During the first week of the term I demonstrated this process for them.

1 I read a short novel to the class, *Looking Out for Sampson*, by Libby Hathorn.

2 What were the purposes for writing book reviews? Why were they useful? This class discussion promoted the idea of publishing a reference book of the book reviews they would write.

3 We discussed the information a book review might contain, using what we knew of *Looking Out for Sampson* — the title, author, publisher, type of book, story content, what did the children think about the book, would they recommend it to others to read, and how would their opinion of the book influence the review they wrote of it.

4 When we had some preliminary planning notes for the review, I began to write it, making sure I wrote on large paper, so all children could see clearly.

5 I verbalised *all* my thinking, explaining the rationale behind what I wrote. I demonstrated my personal editing skills, making changes that I thought were warranted, crossing out and rewriting parts I felt unhappy about and explaining why I thought these were unsatisfactory.

6 I sought conferencing advice and opinion from the children, the editors, and made changes because of this advice if I thought it was justified.

7 I published the final copy of the review as a wall chart and displayed all the drafts as reference for the children's own review writing.

LOOKING AT WRITING FROM A TOPIC LIST

The children had followed their own interests and ideas when choosing the titles to put on the workshop topic list. I then took those titles and built further tasks around them.

'The greatest danger of summer is...'

Children had chosen the title, 'The greatest danger of summer is...' because there had been a recent shark attack on surfers at a nearby beach. They were concerned about the safety of local swimming beaches and wanted to write about this. Because I wanted to be sure that they would look at other safety issues for summer living, I scheduled whole class sessions to investigate these.

I began by reading publications from an Anti-Cancer Council campaign to make children aware of the hazards of sunburn, and the need to wear protection against the sun, especially during the middle of the day. As a senior group in the school, it was important for them to model personal responsibility for their own protection against the sun to younger children in the school.

◆

The initial focus for this topic was reading and discussing an article from a weekend magazine about sunburn, sunscreens and skin cancer — types, causes, and effects. An initial discussion session revealed that the class as a group knew very little about any of these things. After two weeks of enquiring into the subject, most children were able to answer an Anti-Cancer Council questionnaire about the topic successfully.

More importantly, they were all wearing hats during outdoor activities, and younger children were beginning to wear them too.

Some children had investigated other summer hazards, the prevalence of snakes and venomous insects, for example. Others had looked at the danger of bushfires.

If children chose to use this title for one of their pieces of writing, I could find out what information they had collected about it by looking at their writing. I could easily see which children were prepared and able to take their own investigative steps.

Children's work (Des)

THE GREATEST DANGER OF SUMMER IS ....

'Ouch!' I said, as I rolled over. This sunburn was making me suffer. Every time I moved every part of my body felt like it was on fire.

Yesterday I was at the beach all day, tanning and never going in the water once. I went with my friend Kathy. We did nothing but lie in the sun. Kathy put 15+ sunscreen on, and a t-shirt and a hat about 11.00. After a while, Kathy went up under the trees in the park across the road. At the time I laughed at her but now I regret it.

While I was on the beach I fell into a deep sleep. I was dreaming of my future boyfriend. Suddenly I woke. I felt like I was on fire. I looked at my skin. Instead of being a deep brown, it was bright red. My sunscreen only worked for about half an hour, and I had been asleep for over two hours. I know I should have put on a hat and a t-shirt, but I didn't want to be a dag. I looked at my sunscreen, and wished it had been 15+ instead of 8+. I wished I had gone to the park with Kathy. I picked up my things and started to slowly walk over to the park. Then I remembered a show I had seen at school about skin cancer. If you sunburn there was a fair chance of getting skin cancer.

When I reached the park I showed Kathy my sunburn. Instead of her saying, 'I told you so', she gave me a lot of sympathy and took me home!

So here I am, lying in bed in complete agony.

Sunburn is a great danger of summer.

Children's work (Emily)

Both Emily and Des chose to write about the danger of over-exposure to the sun in summer, but they used quite different approaches.

Emily chose to set her information in a fictional narrative, Des kept to the facts. Both pieces of writing were published in the school newsletter, demonstrating to the whole school community how much it was valued.

'My favourite summer treat and how to make it'

This title was expanded into a series of whole class activities, so that children would have a real reason to write about food.

The first step was to demonstrate the common format used to write recipes by writing my own favourite summer treat recipe with them. I always plan to support children's learning by providing a model which they can confidently use for their own work.

The school had a policy of encouraging good nutritional practices, and preparing nutritional food was a regular part of a nutrition program. Children's work on their favourite summer treat recipes was incorporated into this school program.

The recipes were displayed in the classroom and an opinion poll was conducted by the class to determine which recipes were the **class** favourites. The winning four recipes were chosen to be prepared for a class lunch at the end of the workshop period. Two purposes were met here — how to conduct, record and read the results of an opinion poll, and how to prepare food using recipes.

A class recipe book was published, using all the recipes from the group. Value was given to all published recipes by including them in the book, whether they were used for the lunch menu or not.

Once again, the children's activities were publicised: two children wrote about the lunch to include in the school's weekly newsletter.

YESTERDAY, YEAR 6 had a nutrition
session. We ate submarines
(rolls split in half, and baked
with a delicious topping of
tomato, salami and grated cheese)
and lettuce cup salads, followed
by fruit salad. We drank apple
fruit juice sodas. These recipes
were invented by 2 of our class
members - Chonet Adams and David
Brown-Welsh. We thought the
submarines were the best.
Probably most of the class would
agree. The class was divided
into groups and each groups
prepared one item for the rest of
us. Our thanks to group 4 who
did the clearing and washing up.

Darren Tsang and Ben Levett

Newsletter item (Darren and Ben)

At the end of this workshop, only a few weeks into the school year, I had begun to learn quite a lot about each child in my class. As I acquired information about them, I jotted it down, building up a core of knowledge that I could use as a base for the rest of the year's work with them. Many of the ways I used to collect this information are discussed in chapter ten.

WHAT HAD I FOUND OUT?
CHILDREN'S LITERACY SKILLS
I had information about their reading, for example:

1 Capabilities: at what reading level were they, were reading cues integrated?
2 Interests and experiences: because I now have some ideas about what they are interested in reading, what reading materials would be valuable to have as part of the class library?
3 Opinions: were they able to express them?
4 Levels of understanding of texts: were they making inferences about the texts they were reading that they could apply to other texts and other experiences?
5 Approaches to fiction and factual texts: were they able to change their reading style to suit differences in text?
6 Powers of recall and retelling: how accurate were they, were they getting the main idea from the texts they were reading?

I had information about their writing:

1 Capabilities: what type of writing were they most comfortable using? What did I need to demonstrate? What skills would they need to acquire to expand their writing repertoires?
2 Interests and experiences: could they share their experiences, writing with clarity and explaining to their readers?

3 Opinions: could they express their thoughts and feelings?

4 Levels of development of spelling, handwriting, standard writing conventions?

5 Could they accept the challenge of proceeding through each step of the writing process: planning, drafting, editing, to final publication?

CHILDREN'S INFORMATION-GATHERING SKILLS

I had jotted down some information about how the children gathered information, and how they processed it. The children and I would be able to use this information to set learning goals and plan activities for the future.

I had particularly noted children's:
> research skills
> planning and organising information skills
> ability to explain
> recording and presenting skills
> personal experiences they brought to learning tasks
> listening and speaking skills

CHILDREN'S SOCIAL SKILLS

I was interested in children's co-operative skills when working in groups, for instance, while cooking their lunch. I wanted them to recognise the advantages of sharing ideas, talents and skills.

I was beginning to understand them, as individuals. I had observed their working habits and attitudes, how they set their goals and how they achieved them, the responsibility they were prepared to accept for their learning.

I had drawn some conclusions about what they thought of themselves as learners; who felt confident, who did not.

Lastly, I had ideas about their acquisition of the content of the topic they had researched, and the depth of their understandings about that content. I had their products to guide me here. I had talked and listened, trying to get a feel for other topics that would interest them and that they would like to investigate.

The children, too, had made gains during the course of the 'Summertime' workshop.

- They had confirmed that they needed to read and write so that other tasks could be done, for example:

  1 They had read at least one book, and then written a review to be included in a classroom reference.

  2 They had written an independent story for others to read.

  3 They had read to obtain information in order to write, for example, reading recipe books to find a favourite recipe, and then writing it for others to read. They then used it again, to read to

prepare their own lunch, and to make a class recipe book. Their learning had definitely been interrelated here.

4 They had written to give information to others, for example, their recommendations to others about sun safety, and book reviews.

Because all their writing was to be read by others, the need to use standard conventions, correct spelling and legible handwriting was reinforced to them.

- They were made aware that they were continuing to develop expertise with language. Their products had been looked at by others, who had successfully decoded their message.
- They had performed individual and group tasks producing results for real purposes:

1 They had written a class recipe book that had been used for preparing food.

2 They had written a reference book reviewing books that their classmates would most likely enjoy reading.

3 They had conducted an opinion poll to find out class food preferences so that they could prepare a meal that would be enjoyed by most of the group.

4 They had contributed news items and published useful information about sun safety in the school newsletter.

5 They had prepared and eaten a lunch together, relaxing in a sociable activity that would help them establish and build group bonds.

6 They all had the satisfaction of pursuing a writing task to publication, and seeing others in the class read their writing.

7 They were aware of sun safety, accepting personal responsibility for skin protection as a result of their own research.

- They could see that in this classroom there were reasons to learn.
- They understood that their learning was valuable, because the reasons were real.

6

DEMONSTRATING LEARNING

Demonstration is a most powerful teaching strategy. I feel that if I'm not doing it, I can't expect others to. At school, whatever activities I am engaged in, I know the children are watching and learning, so I must consistently show the behaviours I value if I want the children in my care to have those behaviours and value them in themselves and others.

What am I demonstrating if I yell at the top of my voice for the class to 'be quiet'?

That lung capacity wins?

That I want the children to do as I say, not as I do?

We all know that it doesn't work. I'm certainly not demonstrating the notion that quiet is valuable if I am not quiet myself. If I want peace and quiet, I must be quiet. If I want children to write, I must write. If I want children to read, I must read.

I am always conscious that I am a model for young children, particularly, of course, in the classroom. It is here that I am not only demonstrating appropriate learning behaviours. I am, for better or worse, also demonstrating learning expertise.

I would not be doing my job as a teacher, if I did not also demonstrate to the children *how* I became an expert.

DEMONSTRATING THE WRITING PROCESS

Older children in upper primary school classes like to know that it is the same hard struggle for adults to write as it is for them. I make sure they learn this lesson very well.

I like to show them a series of drafts written by myself or another adult, especially if the adult is not in a profession that has writing as an obvious job skill.

Children who feel they will not need to write because they are going to be bricklayers or hairdressers when they grow up might just change their minds when they realise that *all* adults need to write.

Adults, especially parents of children at the school, who can come into the classroom to talk personally about their writing are great models.

This particular series of drafts was written by someone who did not realise at the time that he was demonstrating the writing process.

1 PRE-WRITING: NOTE TAKING
It is essential to have enough information

Pre-writing notes

Here is our adult writer, struggling with pre-writing planning, note-taking, jotting down his ideas, ordering them to clarify and plan his writing sequence, organising, changing his mind, looking at his information, checking all the time.

2 DRAFTING
The meaning becomes clearer as you write

Draft one

54

In his first draft, the writer develops an introduction, clarifying meaning by writing it the best way, and sequences his ideas and information into logical order.

3 DRAFTING
Draft two does not mean a copy of draft one

ESIS or MANAGEMENT.

The Early Separation Incentive Scheme (ESIS) has now come and gone at the time this Bulletin goes to press those people, to leave in July have

---

Draft two

By the time he is working on draft two, the writer has his intentions for the piece mostly under control. Refining, rephrasing, checking conventions of spelling, punctuation and grammar are occupying him now.

4 DRAFTING
Do we ever write the perfect copy?

ESIS or MANAGEMENT

The Early Separation Incentive Scheme (ESIS) has now come and gone. At the time this Bulletin goes to press those people wishing to leave in July have been notified of their retirement.

Draft three

Even at the point of submission for publication, changes can still be made as the writer strives for his best effort.

What have we demonstrated about the writing process by looking at this series of adult drafts with the children?

- The process of writing is similar for everybody.
- Writing follows a sequence:
  pre-writing
  drafting and editing
  publication
- Information and ideas are essential for writing. It is therefore necessary for writers to read widely, exploring and researching their ideas as a basis for their writing.

- Note-taking clarifies ideas, and helps the writer to sequence and order information.
- First drafts concentrate on meaning, which becomes clearer as you write. Later drafts look at language and its conventions.
- Drafting does not mean copying previous drafts.
- The author controls the writing right to the end. He can make changes even at publication stage.

DO IT YOURSELF

Demonstrating writing is simple, and has the added bonus of letting children know, first hand, at the *actual time of writing* , what I, the author am thinking about as I write. I share with the children an incident that has recently happened to me, which might be an idea for a story.

1 WHERE DID I GET MY IDEA? WHAT DO YOU THINK OF MY IDEA?

I'm thinking of writing a story about a funny thing that happened to me in my garden; well, it wasn't funny at the time!

I have some great strawberries growing this year, but every afternoon when I went to pick some, I found that some had been nibbled. I WAS getting angry about it, but this afternoon I finally discovered what had been happening to them.

At first I thought that slaters had been eating them, then I thought it was my chickens getting out and pecking at them, or birds. But yesterday, I was out in the garden, picking the strawberries, and feeling mad about the bites in them, when I saw a head peering out from under some strawberry leaves. It was a snake! And I had nearly touched it! I'd just reached in there to get a strawberry, and I must have been SO CLOSE to that head!

I ran to the fence, waiting for the snake to go away and it came slowly out of the strawberries, towards me at the fence, and it was a goanna!

After I was back in my kitchen having some coffee, I began to think it was funny.

2 PRE-WRITING
What do I need to find out? Who will be my readers?

Pre-writing sample (teacher writing)

I invite the children to help me clarify and organise my thinking about the story, and I share my ideas about an audience to write for by demonstrating the questions and thoughts that I have.

Will I write it about myself? Will I say, 'I went out to my garden', or 'Mrs Gordon went out to her garden', or 'Mary-ann went out to her garden'? I will find it hard to draw bugs, chickens, me, the goanna. Do goannas eat fruit? Was it really him? I thought goannas were carnivorous. Maybe they like sweet things as well.

How do you spell 'carnivorous'? Where's my dictionary?

Who am I writing this for? Who would be interested in reading a story like this? I think I'll make this a picture story book for about Year 1 children, so I'll keep it simple.

3 DRAFT ONE
I own this writing, I can change it as I go

A SNAKE WAS IN THE STRAW-
BERRY(IES) PATCH ! ~~She could see its fat~~ She had nearly touched
~~brown~~ (its) striped scaly body. It moved.
It moved to the edge of the
strawberry patch.

Draft one sample (teacher writing)

I demonstrate and involve the children in my drafting process, thinking out aloud as I go.

Slaters or bugs? I'd better write bugs, because some little children might not know what slaters are.

'She could see its fat, brown, scaly body' — does that sound okay?

4 DRAFT TWO
How does this story sound to you?

A SNAKE WAS IN THE
STRAWBERRIES ! She had NEARLY
touched its ~~striped scaly body!~~
scaly stripes

Draft two sample (teacher writing)

I can continue to redraft as many times as I feel is necessary, right up to the time of publishing.

I'll need to rearrange this part. I will write 'scaly stripes', not 'body'. The last page will just have the goanna. 'Carnivorous' does have an 'o'.

She looked under/underneath? the last clump of leaves. I think I will write 'under', not 'underneath': it sounds better.

5 PUBLICATION
This is the final draft, I have thought of a title at last!

The final draft (teacher writing)

I'm going to draw strawberries on every page, all over the pages, and I'll put the bugs and chickens in as well. I'll have a red cover. I'll type in the text after I draw the pictures.

This type of first-hand demonstration of the writing process is very powerful. The 'stream of consciousness' talk, the 'this is exactly what I am thinking as I write' gives children the understanding that writing is a thinking process, not just a question of the hand holding the pen. They see that effort and attention are required for successful writing. They have seen me 'tell all':
• why I am writing
• what I am writing
• how I am going about the writing
• what will happen to the writing
• when I hope to finish it
• how I want the writing to be received
• whom I am writing for

They have seen me reread the writing periodically as I write, checking its progress, considering changes I might make, why I might make them, and how they will affect the writing and the story outcomes. Having seen the framework, they can use it to construct their own pieces of writing.

Some children in the class are happy to demonstrate their writing to the rest of the class in the same way. I encourage them; peer modelling is very effective.

I not only demonstrate fiction writing. I want the children to know all the purposes for writing, and all the forms writing can take. I want them to realise that the writing process is the same for all writing tasks: reports, poetry, summaries, diaries, observations, letters, labels, invitations, charts, recipes, scripts, directions, minutes of meetings, journals, research findings, descriptions, instructions, rules, programs, lists, reviews, advertisements, questionnaires, jokes, speculations. In fact, whenever I am writing in the classroom, I am demonstrating the process.

How do I know if my demonstrations are successful? By looking at the children's products, and by listening to them as they write.

LOOKING AT CHILDREN'S WRITING

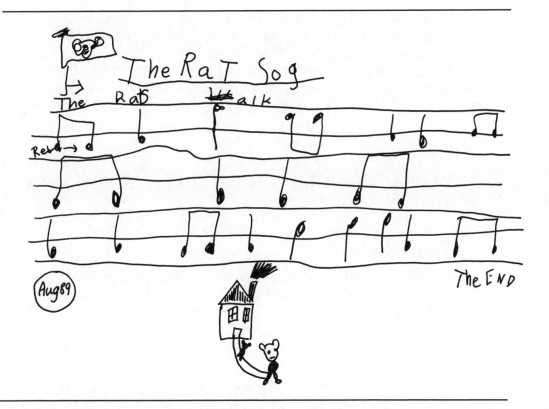

Matthew's writing: The Rat Song

The class had been learning a song, written up using correct musical notation while they watched. This page is taken from Matthew's first draft book where, one week later, he is practising musical notation as a writing form.

Matthew's writing: dinner menu

The class had planned and prepared a lunch, writing shopping lists, recipes, and menus as part of the unit. 'I wrote a menu for our dinner last night,' said Matthew. 'Theis is wot you get,' [This is what you get] he wrote on the bottom of his menu. His writing tells us that he paid close attention to the class lunch activities, learning exactly what is meant by 'menu'. He knows that menus are written as a list, and they are usually decoratively illustrated, hence his use of scrolls and other pictures.

DEMONSTRATING THE READING PROCESS

USSR: A TIME TO READ WITH THE CHILDREN

Probably one of the great times in the school day, especially for the teacher, is USSR — uninterrupted, sustained, silent reading time.

I *always* read as well as the children during this time, because I am expecting children to do as I do. So, I sit there, making myself comfortable, and catch up on my novels (for first choice), journals, references, magazines, newspapers, children's books, books recommended by children, junk mail, flyers, reports, ministrivia, and whatever else may have been cramming my pigeon-hole. Of course, I *know* I'm working — I'm demonstrating:

- how to read silently
- how to read for a sustained period
- how to read for different purposes
- how to read different texts
- how to enjoy reading — I laugh, I cry, I grimace, I throw aside in disgust, I reread
- how to read with enthusiasm

CLASS SERIAL READING: A TIME TO READ FOR THE CHILDREN

Every day I make sure I read a little of the class serial book to my class. I try to make my reading of it as expressive and faithful to meaning as possible: in the classroom, I am the 'expert' reader, and I must keep my reputation intact.

This activity cuts across all other class activities and quite often the book being read as a serial will have a theme that ties in with the topic being studied at the time, and this is a bonus.

I choose books for the children to review for serial reading very carefully, as I am aware that I am demonstrating a number of behaviours here:
- how a good reader chooses a book to read
- what a good reader considers is a good book
- how a good reader expresses an opinion about a book

Once a book for serial reading is chosen, I am conscious that I must demonstrate how a good reader reads and responds to reading.

RESPONDING TO READING

Once a fortnight, the children in my class and I have a literary circle session. We review books we have read, and recommend them or not to others. We read extracts of the 'best bits', we might make posters or 'come-ons' if the book is *really* good. We retell stories, we list astonishing facts from our non-fiction reading.

We tell the jokes, explain the 'how to make' instructions, talk about other books in the series, ask who has them for borrowing and lending, discuss the authors, make collections and lists of related books and materials, read the plays (especially if they are funny), dress up as the characters, try the recipes, put our names on the 'waiting to borrow' list. If we have a book to discuss at these sessions, we have to put our names down on the session agenda sheet before it fills up.

Initially, of course, I am quite often the only performer at these sessions. As the idea takes hold however, I find that I need to put my name down early if I want to discuss my own latest favourite book.

Have my demonstrations been successful? Are the children reading? And what are the children reading? Quite often, books recommended by the teacher and the children in the literary circle sessions.

DEMONSTRATING ORACY

Children are always speaking and listening in my classroom too. Talk is an important part of learning and therefore valued in the workshop classroom.

I allow time and opportunity for speaking and listening to occur, and I demonstrate its importance by giving my full attention to children speaking to me and responding thoughtfully to them. I do not try to surreptitiously soak those rock hard PVA brushes, or glance at the latest directives from the ministry while a child is talking to me.

I listen positively. My reward is to understand the children more, and to build a sound relationship with them.

DEMONSTRATING THAT LEARNING IS VALUED

What value am I placing on children's time if I tap them on the shoulder in the middle of a writing session and ask them to stack some papers that have become disordered, or pop down to the office for some paper clips, or take the lunch orders to the canteen? What am I demonstrating?

I am saying: What you are doing is not very important, you can pick up your thoughts when you get back, this time is not valuable for you, your work is not valuable to me.

I could give a different message if I stacked the papers and let the children continue writing, or waited for a break to fetch the clips or take the lunch orders to the canteen.

I would then be saying: What you are doing is too important to interrupt, I value what you are doing, it is important that you keep going.

PART THREE

ALLOWING LEARNERS TO FUNCTION AT THEIR FULL POTENTIAL

7

TAKING
RESPONSIBILITY

◆

When do we know that a child is taking responsibility for what they are learning? How do we know when children are self-motivated and are prepared to pursue a task because they have good reasons of their own for doing so?

As teachers, our first duty is to carefully observe each child to find out what reason they have for what they are doing.

OBSERVING RESPONSIBLE WRITERS

It was one of the great days for Matthew, aged six years, and in Year 1, when his father finally remembered to bring home a microscope from work. He had been wanting to use a microscope for some time: ever since he had known about them in fact. He wanted to investigate a few things — his own hair, skin and nails, and some of his blood — Matthew the scientist rose to the task. He made his slides and began his study. He had a wonderful time. He was being as careful as he knew how, adjusting and tinkering with the microscope, and he was just taking another look at a slide smeared with saliva (his own) when disaster struck.

The microscope, balanced on the very edge of the bench, reached the point of no return and toppled onto the floor, breaking the light bulb that was part of the magnification mechanism. Matthew was devastated.

His father had impressed upon him that the microscope was a very delicate and very valuable instrument that needed to be handled with the greatest of care, and he had broken it!

What to do?

The only thing to do was to apologise, and Matthew decided to apologise by letter. There was a rationale behind this decision — Matthew knew that his parents liked to receive letters from people. He liked to receive them himself. Letter writing seemed a very adult thing to do, and his father might be pleased and appeased by receiving a letter from him. He set to work drafting a letter during personal writing time in his classroom the next day.

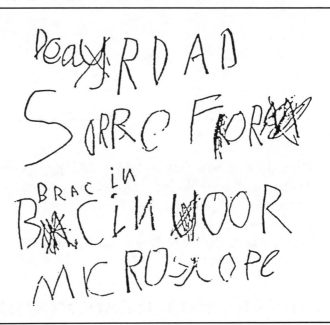

Matthew's letter: draft one

When he read the draft through he was proud of it. It contained the message that he wanted.

Matthew also knew that writing must be able to be understood by the reader, and that it must therefore follow certain conventions, particularly of spelling. His draft letter needed editing. He knew that he had spelt *microscope* correctly because he had been writing reminder notes to his father about bringing it home for weeks. When he came to another hard *k* sound in *breaking* he naturally used a *c* as he had for the same sound in *microscope*. His teacher pointed out that *breaking* used a *k*, so he changed it.

By the time he came to the same sound again in *microscope* he was a little confused. He hesitated— *c* or *k*? His previous experience with the word *microscope* helped him to make the correct decision — he *knew* how to spell this word!

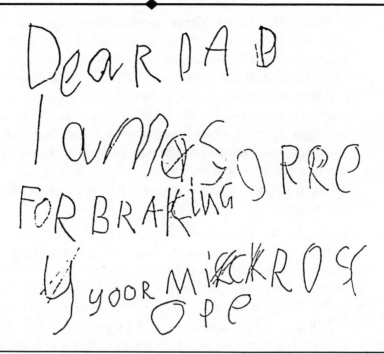

Matthew's letter: draft two

His third draft finally satisfied his understandings of the conventions of spelling. He felt that it used appropriate language and that his father would be able to read it. He decided that this would be the final version.

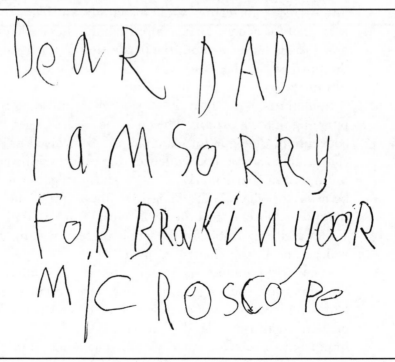

Matthew's letter: draft three

When his father came home, Matthew gave him the letter, confidently expecting that it would be able to be read and that his message would be understood. And this of course is what happened. His father read the letter, and Matthew was forgiven.

Matthew's belief in his ability to use language in an appropriate way was confirmed by his father's reaction to the letter. He had made the right decision when he decided to write the letter, and his success with this gave him the confidence to continue to use writing as a means of communicating with others.

IMPLICATIONS FOR THE TEACHER'S ROLE

As a teacher, I must make certain that all children have the opportunity to pursue their own writing tasks, and are successful with them. The power that comes from writing successfully for personal purposes means children will feel confident about continuing to attempt other writing tasks. 'Nothing succeeds like success' is particularly true for children.

What about the spelling errors in the final draft of Matthew's letter — the one that was given to his father? As a teacher surely my job is to ensure that publication copies are correct in every respect.

Writing that is for general readership obviously should be correct. But in cases like Matthew's, some discretion should be allowed. Matthew was only six years old, a struggling new writer. He had already worked doggedly on three drafts of the letter, and I had helped him correct some errors. Only his family was likely to read the letter; it was not for general readership. I felt that he needed to get that letter home to his father without the frustration of further delay, and before the purpose for the letter was gone. There was plenty of time ahead of him to write perfect final drafts!

Sometimes it is difficult to see what purposes the children are pursuing in their writing. They may be so challenged by a new writing convention, dialogue for example, or so involved in developing their characters to suit a plot sequence, that other writing concerns become unimportant, particularly at the drafting stages of writing. I want to be aware of what children consider important at the time, and allow them to explore, to feel their way without interference or distraction. If they feel responsible for the whole piece of writing, in time children will accept all the challenges in it.

Whenever I am looking at children's writing I am trying to see what the important challenge is that they have accepted. Matthew, in his letter to his father, was conscious that letter writing has conventions of language usage, and that spelling correctly was particularly important. Therefore, this was his challenge, and he accepted the responsibility of drafting and redrafting his letter until he felt he had written the letter correctly.

In another piece of his writing, this challenge did not concern him at all. Here he is writing a story about a character named Beans Baxter (Bes Bacsta), whose gang has met with a spot of bother in a fight with a baddies' gang. The story is called 'The Secret' (The Sekrt), and this is his first draft.

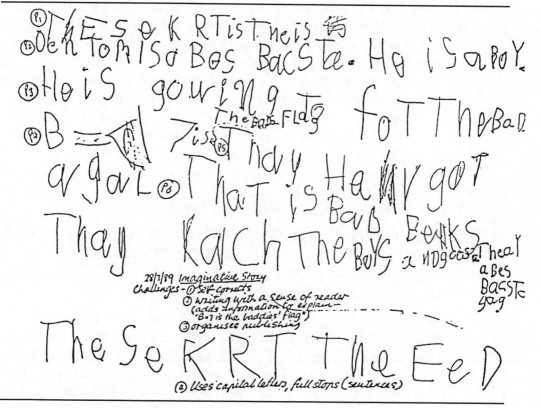

The Sekrt: original draft

The Secret.
The secret is this.
Once upon a time there is Beans Baxter. He is a boy.
He is going to fight the baddies.
B = 7 is the baddies' flag.
They have got a gaol.
That is bad because they catch the boys and girls.
They are Beans Baxter's gang.
The end.

What challenges are important for Matthew in this story? He is drafting a story that he wants to publish as a book to be read by his fellow classmates. He is not concerned with spelling at this stage; he knows that he will need to deal with that later when he comes to his final draft. Now he is trying to clarify his meaning for his readers. He adds extra information: 'B = 7 is the baddies' flag', and 'They are Beans Baxter's gang' so that his readers will be able to distinguish the opposing gangs. He uses sentences with capital letters and full stops to make the reading of the story easier. He works with an editor (me) to organise the story into page-length pieces for his proposed book. He numbers each page. He is planning the story carefully, in order to make it a book, and that is his challenge.

Because I can see that this is his challenge, I can give him the help he needs. I help him organise the writing for publication. I become a 'critical friend' for him, challenging him to continue to clarify the meaning of his story for his future readers.

If I had not investigated his writing carefully, I might have concluded that this piece of work, even though it is a first draft, is 'below' the competency he displayed in his letter writing. Instead, I can see that he has these other purposes in mind, and these observations have changed what I see in his writing.

Besides observing individual children writing, and using my observations to guide me in the help I need to offer to them, I also give more general help to the whole class.

HELPING CHILDREN BECOME RESPONSIBLE FOR THEIR WRITING

I support children through each part of the writing process, dividing the whole writing task into manageable 'chunks'.

HELPING CHILDREN TO PLAN THEIR WRITING

Helping children to plan their writing allows them to accept responsibility for the task while still knowing that they own it. A pre-planning sheet can be a useful tool for them to use when making decisions about their writing. I have used this one with older children from Year 3, but it could be adapted for younger children, and it can be used orally at teacher–child conferences, where the teacher can write down the child's thoughts and ideas as they are discussed.

NAME: Natalie   Before writing:

1. Why have I chosen this topic? I have choosen to do another set piece for my independant writing because it is easyer for me to do a set title plus I couldn't to think of anything else. also I am superstitious

2. Outline (in point form) of my ideas and information I am going to use for this writing:

1. I am going to think of all the superstitions I can!.
2. I am going to write down all the ideas I and think of ways to illustrate them
3. then I am going to do a good copy and sort of make it a test to see if you are superstitious

3. Who will read this? Year six

4. How do I want this writing to affect reader. I want it to make them think a say to themsely's "am I superstitious

Pre-planning sheet for writing

◆

The planning sheet helps children to focus their attention on several pre-writing concerns that they might have.
- What are my reasons for writing about this subject?
- Who will be my audience?
- How will this affect what I write?
- What ideas do I have about this?
- How will I order my information?
- How will I structure the content of the writing?

Jotting down their ideas will help children to clarify them.

HELPING CHILDREN EDIT AND REVISE THEIR WRITING

Editing and revising is difficult for any writer, especially the young and inexperienced. It is hard to focus on your own writing and see where changes might be needed.

In my classroom, I try to give children the help they need for this task, and the experience, by using a system where the children edit each other's writing using an editing diary sheet. When I edit a child's writing, I use the same sheet. By doing this I can demonstrate how to edit to two children at once, the writer and the editor. Here are Danae, Amanda and I editing Melissa's writing.

WORKSHOP DIARY SHEET   NAME: Melissa (AMANDA)

TITLE	DATE, COMMENT	NAME
The best day of the whole holidays	15·2·90 Melissa you have to check your spelling and full stops. And your sentences have to make sense.	Amanda McHugh.
The best day of the whole holidays	15·2·90 Melissa it was good except the Capitals and spelling	Amanda McHugh
The best day of the whole holiday	16·2·90 It was a really good story. fix up spelling and add full stops and commars. Then it will be Terrific!	Danae.
	16·2 Ready to publish paragraphing — one per day in the story. Interesting original content.	Gordon
Book Review	26/2 Really good outline. Needs a reason for opinion though	Danae.
the greatest danger of summer is...	26·2 Great Story! Unusual Ending.	Danae.

Melissa's editing sheet

When I edit children's writing with them, I ask the questions I want children to ask of their own writing.

- Is your meaning clear?
- Will your ideas reach your planned audience?
- Is the story in order? Is it sequenced?
- Is the style suitable for the content?
- Are there paragraphs? Is the punctuation correct?
- What about spelling?
- Here is *my opinion* of your writing.

Children who are editors for their classmates are encouraged to keep editing comments clear and simple, starting with positive statements. I don't want the task of editing to appear too daunting.

By editing each other's writing, children will pick up strategies that will help them look critically at their own writing.

HOW DO I KNOW WHEN CHILDREN FEEL RESPONSIBLE FOR THEIR WRITING?

Certain behaviours distinguish children who are self-motivated writers.

1 They want to write every day. In fact, they are loud in their cries of deprivation if they think they have 'missed out' on a writing session. 'It's not fair!' and 'We *never* get to write!' are catch-cries of responsible writers who feel they have not had a 'fair go'.

2 They are happy to research and develop their own ideas and information for their writing; they want to choose their own writing topic. They are indignant if they are asked to write on a 'set' topic too often. 'Do we *have* to?' is their cry in this situation.

3 Editing is not a chore for the responsible writer, but an opportunity to review and revise, to check that their writing is following the path they intended for it. The name of the responsible writer is the one that is either *always* on your 'waiting for an edit session with you' sheet because they want to explain the editing they have already done or their name is *never* on the sheet because they are revising their story for the thirtieth time and they can't waste time — you can read it when it is published in its bound Moroccan leather cover.

4 Responsible writers are more than delighted to present their writing to their audience — to share, read aloud, send to, publish for, to *use* as they had intended it to be. They may be happy to do this every day if they are allowed, and if time permits.

OBSERVING RESPONSIBLE READERS

I once had an avid reader who suddenly stopped reading in class, to my concern, and at home, to his parents' distress. After watching him browsing listlessly through books and magazines during reading sessions for a week or two, casting books aside, 'forgetting' to take books home to read, or to bring his library books back, I asked Ben what his problem was.

He shuffled about, answering questions without enthusiasm, volunteering nothing. I asked him about his library borrowing lately. His story started to emerge, until finally he burst out, 'I hate the librarian at this school!'

'Uh oh,' I thought. 'A personality clash. I'll have to hasten slowly here.' And a rather sad story unfolded.

'I can only take out two books a day,' Ben complained. When I pointed out that two books a day was really ten a week, surely enough reading, he agreed, but...

'When I borrow two books one day, and bring them back the next morning, *she* says I can't possibly have read two books in one night. I hate going back when she says that, so I don't go.'

Ergo, I don't read!

Who is making decisions here about what reading this child does! It is important to allow children to take responsibility for *how much* reading they wish to do as well as *what* they wish to read.

A lot of children appear to go through periods of 'binge' reading when they want to read anything and everything, and do very little else during these times. Other children will only read those books that are appealing at a particular time; for example, they may only read 'choose your own adventure' books, and when they have read them all, they stop reading altogether for a while until they develop a crush on another type of book, and then off they go again.

Some children read and reread the same book over and over — or only the work of one author. When presented with something else to read, they may resist to the point of not reading at all.

In the classroom, I like to give children sole responsibility for choosing what they read and how much they read. This is not to say that I do nothing about their reading at all. I do many things, all of them essential to help children become responsible readers.

1 I observe them and their reading, collecting information about their reading behaviours. The responsible reader has particular characteristics, and I want to know which children are responsible readers, so I look for those characteristics:

- Responsible readers are very keen to read.
- They look forward to reading sessions.
- They are content to choose what they read.
- They are happy to talk about their reading, to review and share their responses to a book with others.
- If they are attempting to read a more difficult text than they would normally choose, or read more than is usual for them, they are

ready for that challenge, despite what others might think.

2 I encourage reading by demonstrating the pleasures of reading:
- I read to myself
- I read to the children
- I talk about new or interesting books, maybe in a 'literary circle' time

3 I encourage children to review and share their reading in many different ways, for example, readers theatre sessions, read and retell, art and craft activities, performances, etc.

4 I encourage newly independent readers in particular to keep a tally of the books they have read. Children are great collectors. Some like to collect matchbox cars or stickers, others like to collect the titles of the books they have read. I try to cash in on this and provide a carefully designed tally sheet with the option of including a brief opinion on each book read. Children can choose to fill these in or not, but I do allow time for them to do so.

I HAVE READ...

TITLE OF BOOK, AUTHOR OF BOOK	START	FINISH	WHAT DID I THINK OF IT

Reading tally sheet

5 I allow a lot of time for reading, giving value to it by ensuring that it is timetabled every day. I never say, 'Close your book and pack up now,' to the children — I know how frustrated I feel if I am not allowed the time to finish the part I am reading. Therefore I say, 'We'll finish in about five minutes, ' or, 'Meet me in our conference space at twelve-fifteen.' Responsibility is given to each child to finish and pack up within that time — plenty to wind up their reading at a suitable break.

6 If I observe children who are not reading independently, I take more positive action. I strike while the iron is hot — one of my favoured teaching strategies. I talk to them about their reading, asking what they like to read, and I bring them the latest book by their favourite author. I suggest another book, related to the one they have just been reading; I pair them with another child with the same reading interests; I bring snippets of information, reviews or magazine articles about the books they like to read; and I stockpile books I know children are reading at the moment.

I am consciously *not* taking the responsibility for the reading away from the children; I am helping their developing independence.

7 I ensure that all the people involved with the children in my class are aware that the children have responsibility for their own reading.

Dear Parents,

One of our educational objectives is to encourage the children to become independent and responsible learners, and one of the ways to achieve this is to let children decide about their learning tasks.

The home reading scheme is part of our program planned to encourage children to take responsibility for decisions about their reading.

Children will choose their own books for home reading, and write the name of the book and the date they borrow it in their reading record books. Please sign their record books and add any comments when books have been read.

Children may like to discuss your comments about their reading with you or add comments of their own. Don't worry if your child takes time to work out which books are right for his/her reading. This is part of the decision-making process!

If you have any queries please pop in and see me.

Dale Gordon.

Letter to parents about reading

I remind myself all the time that learners themselves are the only ones who can do their own learning. The motivation to learn, and the direction the learning takes, is a shared responsibility in the classroom, but ultimately they must decide what they learn, how much they learn and when they will learn it.

8

APPROXIMATION

Even in a classroom with ideal learning conditions, children's language skills will develop slowly and randomly.

It is rewarding to monitor their progress, observing their moves from task to task, becoming aware of the challenges they accept as they make their way towards language competency, and looking at the changes in their products as they test and confirm their experimental actions. It is a privilege to witness children's private battle towards independent learning, to be taken into their confidence as a mentor who will guide and counsel, and as a friend who will accept and celebrate.

It is important have a clear general understanding of how children's language develops. It is possible to read about this, as there are a great many books available on the subject. However, it is also essential to spend a lot of time observing children at work and discussing your observations with them and with other teachers, building expertise by direct experience. It is important to be able to monitor effectively and intervene appropriately in the language development of each child in the classroom.

In order to begin to appreciate the language development made by children, I look at their language products over as long a period of time as I can. I like to see where their present learning fits into their long-term learning progress. It would be an advantage to have records for the whole of each child's schooling. Many schools have taken up this type of record-keeping, using profiling methods.

It is interesting to make a longitudinal study of one child's progress yourself, looking at the child's steps over a number of years. The insights gained by making this study are invaluable. It is particularly easy to keep samples of writing development.

LOOKING AT ONE CHILD'S WRITING
MATTHEW BEGINS TO WRITE

The perseverance of the beginning writer is awe-inspiring. From the start, the beginning writer accepts the responsibilities that every writer faces, and endeavours to reconcile a written product with known understandings of the written language. The child *is* a writer from the first attempt, and from that first moment, strives to closely approximate the conventions of formal writing.

'I did my writing'

Even before Matthew, aged four, could write conventional letter shapes, he was demonstrating that he had understandings about written language, and he was prepared to use his understandings to communicate by writing. He knew that messages could be written; he had asked people to be his scribe and write his messages for him, and he had registered that his messages could be read back. He had observed people around him engaged in their own writing tasks — 'I did my writing,' his inference being 'just like you'.

He demonstrated what he knew so far about the conventions of written language: writing is composed of discrete shapes that go together; writing has sequence, from left to right, from top to bottom in straight lines.

'I am writing about my house'

A couple of months passed, and Matthew began to write to give readers information, his information: 'I am writing about my house.' He saw that, as the writer, he could choose what his message would be. He began to use some conventions of letter shapes, M (for Matthew), dotted strokes, circle shapes, joined zigzag shapes.

'This is Matthew's homework'

Using the letters that made up his own name, Matthew did his 'homework', just like his older siblings, who were his 'teachers' at this stage, busy with their own homework, and demonstrating this purpose for writing to him.

He knows now that there is a difference between writing and drawing, and he uses only writing for his 'homework', just like his models.

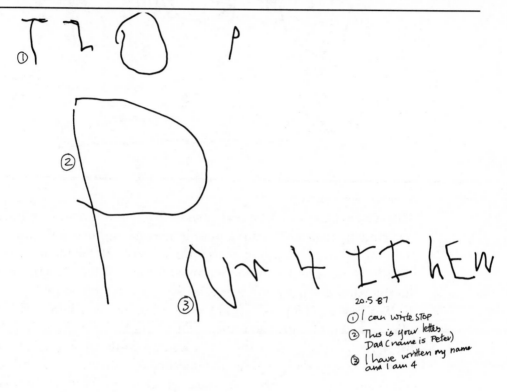

'I can write stop'

Matthew had become very aware of the writing in his environment: stop signs and other road signs, name tags on his clothing, books, advertisements, television. He read anything. He was becoming very interested in discrete letters, and his favourite spot was in front of the refrigerator which was covered in magnetic letters, numbers and other shapes. He began to appreciate graphophonic connections: 'This is your letter Dad,' he said as he wrote a large letter *P* for Peter on the page. He realised that the message contained in a group of letters could not change; 'I can write "stop", ' (just like the sign at the end of the road). He wrote his name, and put a 4 in it, because 'I am four.'

When other people could read his writing back to him, his own beliefs about the accuracy of the conventions that he was using were confirmed, and he was given the encouragement to continue to persevere with the use of them.

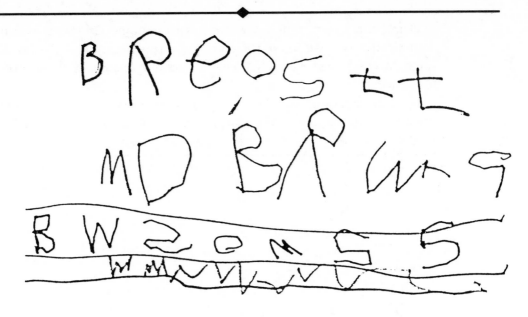

'A red bat and a blue ball'

By Christmas, when he had turned five, Matthew was prepared to experiment, using his graphophonic knowledge to write some more 'homework'. In his first line of writing he wrote *Re* for *red* and the final *t* of *bat*. In his second line he wrote *nd* for *and*, *B* for *blue*. In his third line he tried a short sentence: *Some boys play*. By the time he reached the 'last line' on the page, he was exhausted, and concluded with some 'filler' pattern of zigzagged lines: 'This is just writing,' he said. What effort he used to match these few sounds with the right letters!

Matthew was also prepared to experiment with other types of written communication he saw in his environment. In January he became interested in No Smoking signs, and he experimented with a few signs of his own: No Guns, No Robbers, No Cannons, No Cigarettes, No Spears.

'No signs'

'I see a monster. Do you?'

At school at last, Matthew was now prepared to accept the challenge of choosing a topic and writing about it. He was happy for the moment with his mastery of graphophonic conventions. He continued to approximate conventional spelling. Stories had became important to him, and he was using his imagination to write them.

'Matthew is the boss of the room'

Matthew was writing here for a definite purpose — this is MY territory! He intended to inform his readers of this, so he spent some time ensuring that he was using conventional language that could be understood readily by everyone.

'This is my dad. He likes to help build my castle.'

At first glance, this piece of writing displayed less mastery of written language conventions than that shown in Matthew's writing six months before. Apart from 'dad' and 'my', he used only initial consonants to represent words, and he had even written the first line from right to left, something that he had rarely done at all in the past.

One of the advantages of looking at the development made by a child over a long period of time is learning that language development does not proceed in a smooth upward curve. This is an important piece of information to keep in the back of one's mind at all times in the classroom, where we only see the development of each child over the short period of time in one school year.

MyFaRTfeiⁿⱮ   My favorite things

iSⱭeR M
ⱭoST BooK

Mycais   My cars
BooD SHoS   boardshorts

PLa   play
Bosm
SWM   beach

Caot DRayLa   Count Dracula

my ToP HaiS   My top house
LemⱤaP

'My favourite things'

In his second year at school, Matthew was experimenting again, this time with layout, as he wrote for a new purpose, to list his favourite things of the moment. He was beginning to feel confident about some sound groups — *oo, sh, ing*. This would be an appropriate time for his classroom teacher to demonstrate blended sounds to him, and to help him build a reference list of words containing these sounds.

WaS TheReWaS a KaSooL
aNDTheReWe a MeⱧ
aⱧD The KⁿⱲ -MDa QeⱧ
thaTLⱸVDi ⱵKaSooL
TⱧeReWaS a DⱤo en
aⱧDTⱨⱲa FoTDTheDⱤaⱧ
aⱧDThaLeVD HPaLe

Once there was a castle,
and there was men
and the king and queen
that lived in the castle.
There was a dragon,
and they fought the dragon.
And they lived happily.

'The castle'

I know about dinosaurs.
I think they
blow fire.
And they have teeth.
And they are dangerous.
They are very dangerous.
They eat meat.
They eat other dinosaurs.

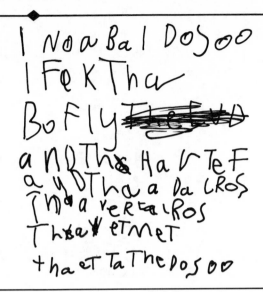

'Dinosaurs'

Matthew had built up a store of information about the language used in books. He was a great listener of stories, and he knew that in fairytales he could expect to read phrases like 'once upon a time', and 'happily ever after'. He knew that fairytales were likely to be about dragons and kings and queens and other fanciful characters. Settings might be romantic, and the plot would involve a conflict in which the 'goodies' overcome the 'baddies' and win. His own story, beginning with 'Once there was...' reflected these understandings. He had also had non-fiction texts read to him, and his account listing the characteristics of dinosaurs was written strictly as information for his readers.

I saw Batman. He was
fighting the Riddler. He
kicked and punched and tripped
the Riddler. Batman won.
I go in. I kicked the Riddler.
'Serves you right!' I said.
The Riddler is in gaol, but he
escapes from gaol. But Batman
shot him.

'Batman'

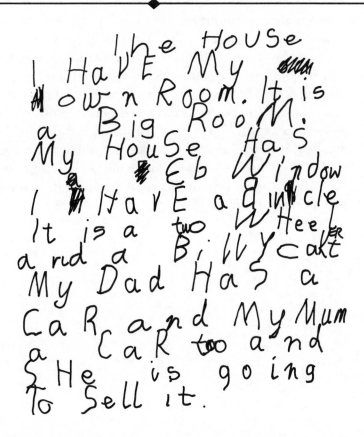

'The house'

As Matthew moved closer towards independence as a writer, he began to think about the content of his writing, the style he would use to suit the purpose of the particular piece, and the conventions of usage expected of a writer. He did all this as he wrote. He corrected conventions, rereading with an editor's eye, planning for his audience and for publication. We can see all this happening as we look at these last two samples of his writing.

His Batman story was a tale of adventure that he intended to publish as a book. He made sure that it had a narrative format, with an introduction followed by a series of actions leading to the climax: 'I go in.' The consequences were revealed in the conclusion: 'Batman shot him.'

'The House', on the other hand, was part of a description of his own life story, almost a diary. He had been very careful with spelling accuracy, as he had not intended to rewrite it or publish it in another form. It was a private list, giving information about himself. If we compare this to his 'Favourite Things' list of less than a year before, it is easy to see the progress he has made in his ability to order his ideas, to spell and to use sentence structures and punctuation.

It is a great achievement for the child, and for the teacher who needs to keep tabs on every child's individual progress!

It can be done, and the keys are **organisation** and **observation**.

It is not easy to organise daily routines and timetables so that the teacher is freed from direct face-to-face teaching for some time each day in order to observe and record observations of children at work. Never lose sight of *why* you are observing children's learning. In a nutshell, it is so that you can use the information you gather to help establish future directions for that child. Keep reminding yourself about this. Observation time is easier to organise if you keep in mind that it is priority number one!

9

EXPECTATIONS FOR LEARNING

———————————◆———————————

A few years ago I was teaching a class of twenty-one Prep children. On their very first day at school there was great excitement, for me as well as the children, as we all began to establish ourselves into a new routine. After morning recess we began to feel settled and adjusted to the novelty of a new environment: tales had been told and stories read, chairs and tables had been tested for size and comfort, cupboards had been investigated, play equipment trialled, and morning tea had been had by all.

BEGINNING WRITING

I asked the children to sit close to me, and to watch what I was doing. 'Writing!', they all-called out as they watched me making marks on my paper. 'Yes,' I said, 'I am writing this — "We are all going to write today". '

It turned out that they all already knew how to write, and they were all very determined to tell me of their experiences with writing too. So we discussed writing, where the children had seen it before, who wrote, what types of writing they were familiar with, what were the purposes for writing, what could be used for writing — types of paper, writing implements, etc. As they gossiped on, as only a Prep class can, I wrote down some of the things they were talking about, reading them out as I wrote, and reading my sentence again too: 'We are all going to write today.' After a while, I gave each child a pencil and an exercise book, writing their names on the covers as I did so, and asked them to start their writing.

Not *one* child did not write. In fact, they all wrote with enthusiasm and confidence.

TRANSCRIBING WRITING

I began transcribing their writing into conventional language with them. I would ask them to read their writing to me, I would transcribe it, and ask them to read my transcription as I pointed to the words. Then we would discuss their future plans for the piece. They went on to illustrate it or to add further writing. It was a great session.

Derek, aged five, came to me with his writing. 'Derek, what a lot of writing you have done! Read me your writing.' I prepared to transcribe.

'No,' said Derek. 'You know how to read, you read it. I can write, but I can't read yet. Read me what I wrote.'

WHAT THE WRITER BRINGS TO THE WRITING SESSION

What does Derek know about writing?

He knows that writing is for readers to read.

He knows that writing has a message that readers can retrieve when they want to.

What expectations has he for his own writing?

He expects that his writing has a message that can be read.

He expects that he can write that message.

He expects that he will eventually be able to read that message but, as he said, 'I can't read it *yet*.'

Are his expectations for himself realistic? After all, at this stage he has had very few formal reading and writing experiences on which to base his expectations for his own development. On what is he basing them, therefore? He bases some of his expectations on his previous learning experiences, the success or failure of them and the feedback he received from them. He sees and understands the expectations that others have for him — his parents, siblings, peers, and now his teacher — and these have made him aware of the expectations he should hold for himself. He measures his beliefs about his capabilities with theirs. If they are a match, he will see that his beliefs are valuable and therefore worth having, and that his expectations for his learning are realistic.

THE TEACHER'S RESPONSIBILITY TO THE WRITER

In the classroom, therefore, I have a responsibility to Derek. I must not only have realistic expectations for him, but I must let him know I have them so that he can confirm his own.

I must project an attitude which says: 'This classroom is a workshop for learning. Learning is valued here. Come in, because I believe you can learn and I will do my best to support you in your learning.'

All the children I have ever known are like Derek. They know they are learners, and they know there is *nothing* they cannot learn. I want them to know that I believe this too. I want them to know that I endorse their expectations for their learning, and that I will be working actively with them to help them meet their expectations.

With this in mind, at the beginning of the school year — day one in fact — I like to discuss with my class what I hope we will achieve individually and as a group during our time together, and to make explicit the expectations we have for our learning.

Last year I looked at the expectations for the year with a Year 6 class. I started with my own expectations, what I hoped I would achieve in the year, my 'new year's resolutions' in fact. I had typed my list before the session, and put it on an overhead transparency — I was demonstrating its importance to me by spending time and effort in its preparation and presentation. My list looked like this:

PERSONAL GOALS FOR 1990

1 To continue my learning by-
   a working with you to help you achieve your learning goals.
   b working with other teachers, particularly in the Western Region, and looking at learning and teaching.
   c reading, writing, talking and listening, and then reflecting on what I read and write, and on the conversations I have about learning.
2 To read for pleasure, especially novels, and to read the newspaper EVERY DAY.
3 To keep fit, by exercising regularly and eating a healthy diet.
4 To keep a journal of my experiences in 1990, and my thoughts about them.

When I had spoken of my own expectations for the year, I asked the children to write down their expectations for their own learning. I allowed about twenty minutes for this — I wanted the children to have time to put all their thoughts down — I wanted them to know that this activity was valued sufficiently highly to have plenty of time allotted to it.

The children were asked to discuss their expectations list with a friend, in pairs. They were to think about:
• what expectations were common to both lists
• why this was so
• what they were surprised to see
• what they would now add to their own list
• what changes of any sort would they make to their own list now

that they had shared another person's ideas

Still in pairs, the children chose an expectation common to them both, or one they considered to be the most valuable, and wrote that one on a class list. We discussed the class list. It was clear that children's expectations for themselves were similar.

Challenge

To keep Learning
To get ready for high school Y7
To improve handwriting
To have fun with learning
To write some excellent stories.

Expectations

To Learn as much as possible
To work harder
To read, and learn from books
To improve our reading skills
To have fun at school
To improve all subjects especiall
y Maths.

Class list of expectations

I showed the children my expectations of them — these had been written on an overhead transparency before the session. We looked to match the class list, developed from children's individual expectations, with mine. It was surprising to the children to discover how closely linked the two lists were. They were now very conscious of what they expected to achieve in terms of their learning, and what a teacher's expectations for their learning might be.

MY EXPECTATIONS OF YOU *******************************

1 To continue your learning by:
  a taking responsibility for your work
        * **independent learner**
  b working with ALL your classmates accepting and giving
     help with learning
        * **co-operative learner**
  c reading every day
     writing every day
     listening and talking for a purpose every day
        * **active learner**
  d reflecting on what you have been
     reading
     writing
     listening to and talking about
        * **reflective learner**
  e keeping fit and healthy by having regular exercise and a
     healthy diet
        * **healthy learner**
  f having a go! At everything!
        * **resourceful, flexible learner!**

2 To become responsible leaders of this school.

3 To be prepared to justify your actions and your behaviours.

As links were made between the two lists — and they were very apparent — something began to happen. The children began to see that there were common goals and expectations child-to-child and child-to-teacher. The first inkling of a truth began to dawn — we were all on the same side! We had common expectations for their learning.

Holding this session on the first day of the school year allowed children to see this match right from the start of our relationship.

We then looked at some specific ways in which these expectations could be achieved.

We thought of experiences and activities that would help meet our expectations and wrote them on a wall list, e.g. 'In order to become better readers we will read every day for at least half an hour,' 'We must produce a completed piece of independent writing each term,' 'In order to become healthy learners we will all bring at least one piece of fruit to eat at school every day,' 'All children must participate in all physical education lessons.'

Once discussed and agreed upon, this list became part of the learning activities planned for the year. Of course, some flexibility was allowed to cater for individual needs and changes in situation, but, generally, they were realistic enough to be suitable for the whole group to perform regularly.

Most importantly, they had been decided by the whole group, for the group, and because this list had been produced co-operatively, the chance that the activities would be performed increased. The more the activities were done, of course, the closer children came to meeting their own learning expectations. For example, if we read every day, we will become more competent readers.

It is important now for the teacher to set up the programs that will help children meet their expectations for their learning.

PROGRAMMING LANGUAGE WORKSHOPS

All of us work more efficiently and effectively when we know what we expect to learn. I like to make sure that the children in my class do know what expectations they might confidently hold for their learning, and they are invariably high.

In one school I taught at, the staff decided each year what topic would be the focus for study for that year. They made the topics very broad, so that they would contain enough to interest every year level and every child.

One year the whole school topic for the year was, 'The society we live in'. I was teaching a Year 6 group that year, and in term one we looked at the composition of our Australian society, and investigated how our society developed its diversity, the personal differences in its members, the effects of immigration, the influence of other cultures, indigenous people, etc.

Our language sessions were focused on this topic too, and we developed a language workshop, based on the work being done in the topic. To give importance to the workshop, it was grandly titled 'Writers' Workshop', and it planned to add to the children's own investigations of their society, and have them study themselves as members of it. Children listed the investigations they would like to make about themselves, and these became titles for a writing folio.

Little Brother by Allan Baillie was selected as a class serial.

The writers' workshop had a number of non-negotiable obligations, put forward by me, and agreed to by the group:
- There was a time limit for completing the workshop.
- Five pieces of completed work were required.
- Presentation of folio counted.
- Writing drafts were essential, and were to be included.
- Editing was essential. An editing sheet was to be used for this purpose.

WRITERS' WORKSHOP: TERM ONE

TITLE: 'ME'

1   During term one you are expected to produce a folio of five pieces of writing.

2   Expectations for the folio:

♦ The folio should include a title page and a general introduction.

♦ Drafts are to be written in your draft books.
Finished pieces are to be published in your folio.

♦ Drafts and finished pieces of writing are to be conferenced by your editor
and your teacher at least once a week.
Any comments are to be entered on your Workshop Diary sheet.

♦ Folios are to be completed by Friday 6 April and handed in with your Workshop
Diary sheet attached.

3   Support work will be done during class language sessions.

4   Choose five titles from the following list. You may choose to write an
independent   piece. (See me.)

a. My most embarrassing moment
b. Games I played when I was young
c. Research piece: My family tree - how far back can you trace your family?
d. Timeline: important events in my life
e. My favourite recipe and how to prepare it
f. 'Let me tell you how to...' knit, play hockey, etc.
g. A plan of my bedroom, to scale, and a plan of the bedroom I would LIKE to
have
h. My future
i. A day in the life of...me
j. An interview with my favourite relative
k. An interesting story about one of my ancestors
l. The family I would like to have

5   All folios will be displayed for reading by others in our school.
Your parents will be invited to see them too.

Writers' workshop, term 1: Me

Children monitored their writing progress using the workshop diary sheet. They selected a friend to be their editor, someone to help them monitor their writing, to make them aware of the paths they were taking and the paths they should plan to take. Editors wrote their comments on the sheet so that a record of consultation was kept. Other interested and/or invited people also added comments, especially, of course, the owner of the writing and the teacher. This was a useful record for conferencing, and for assessing and planning individual children's programs.

WORKSHOP DIARY SHEET.   NAME: Leah (chonét)

TITLE	DATE, COMMENT	NAME
My favorite summer treat	12.2 good but a couple of punctuation	Heidi
The Best Day	A side story. where did you get the idea?	Catherine
Book Review	12.2. Well presented and interesting to read	Natalie
	15.2 Summer treats yum your Check a few spellings.	
Book review	15.2 Ready to publish	
The Best Day	21.2 Content — a charming story well told. Publish	This could be published as a book for class library!
Moving Day	Well written, good content, few spelling mistakes good	
Spelling	illustrator, answered, they'd, superior	
Flies	I could not follow your illustrated diagram	
Snake Story	An imaginative conclusion. Your descriptions of the "lady from next door" make interesting reading. Paragraphing is accurate	
presentation	You have completed all items a, c, d — at least to edited draft stage, and your work is of a high standard. Please publish The Best Day.... and hand in an independent piece of writing (number b) You have an easy writing style that is pleasant to read, and your story ideas are interesting and original	
(5.3) The Martians	: the beginning of a great adventure	

PRESENTATION OF FOLIO: Your front cover is superb.

All items in your folio were attractively presented Maybe you went 'overboard' with the packaging - you probably did not need to make and use the pink folder

Workshop diary sheet

A lot of classwork was done to support the children in their writing. I demonstrated many of the writing forms from the titles list in workshops, and set up opportunities for children to work in small self-supporting groups to experiment with unfamiliar writing forms.

It was a good opportunity for children to try a number of writing forms they might not ordinarily attempt when writing independently. The workshop gave children experience in **researching information** and then:

- representing it diagrammatically, e.g. time lines, room plans, family tree
- writing it as an anecdotal record, e.g. interview, story about an ancestor
- writing directions, i.e., how to do something, e.g. play a game
- ordering and sequencing events, e.g. an embarrassing moment, one day's events

and **projecting themselves** into different social situations, and **recording** their ideas and feelings:

- my future
- changing their family to the family they would like to have

I spent a lot of time demonstrating 'how to' techniques using the writing forms required by the workshops. It was essential for children to feel confident working with them, and to have the expectation that they would achieve success with their tasks and have worthwhile results for their efforts.

I carefully monitored children's progress through the workshop. I accumulated information about their progress using a diary to jot down observations made of their work, collecting samples of work, interviewing children to discuss their progress, recording the main details of our conversations, filing any information that could be useful in my assessment of their progress. I wanted to be aware of the learning processes they used and to build an understanding of their future directions and needs.

The writing titles in the workshop were related to other studies undertaken within the topic. For example, there were a number of links with the book we were reading as a serial. The writing title, 'Let me tell you how to...' was discussed in class when the serial reading of *Little Brother* reached the point where Vithy, the main character, was desperately trying to construct a bike from scrap parts in an attempt to provide himself with some transport for escape. Allan Baillie described how to build a bike in great detail.

During the class support session for the writing title, Baillie's description of the bike building was analysed to find out what writing techniques he used to write this sequence of construction details in such an interesting way, while at the same time giving the reader a lot of information about the process of bike building. His technique of explaining what the boy was thinking about as he built, his hopes and fears for his brother's safety, and his worry that he was not competent enough to build the bike, or that he wouldn't find the bike parts that he needed, or that someone would interfere before he'd finished the building, put interest, and tension, in the story. How could this interwoven and complex story structure of Baillie's be attempted by Year 6 writers?

One way was to draft a procedural text ourselves, attempting to use Baillie's technique, with all the children involved in the writing. The title of the class text became, 'How to write a story', and the whole class was involved from the start — after all, they all had a point of view about this one!

Included in the writing were class members' individual and group thoughts about their own writing, their concerns for this text and their feelings of confidence (or not) in their ability to produce it. Baillie's character Vithy had expressed similar thoughts about his capacity to build a bike.

The class text also offered an explanation of the writing process, just as Baillie explained the process of bike building.

The 'How to write a story' draft was edited until all the co-writers were content. It was important to publish the draft in a form suitable for others to read, perhaps in the school newsletter, or as a reference book in the school library. The children were proud of their efforts in producing this complex text, and wanted others to admire it.

Having been through the process of writing a procedural text as a group, in a shared and therefore non-threatening manner, children picked up understandings of the techniques used by Baillie and, armed with the confidence of knowing what to do, were more likely to attempt to write their own independent 'How to...' text. They would expect, rightfully, that their attempt would be successful.

WHAT HAD I FOUND OUT?

- I knew what the whole group, and some individuals within it, knew about procedural texts.
- I knew what problems some of the children had, and I could address these in future support sessions.
- I knew who would 'have a go' at this title by themselves, and who would feel happier if they could make the attempt with the support of a small co-operative 'expert' group.
- I knew what I could expect to see children doing with this title — what strategies they would employ — probably a variation on the shared writing strategies.

- I knew what understandings they would have of this particular writing form when they came across it next time.

As we worked with the other workshop titles, I collected similar information about the children's understandings. My knowledge of the children continued to build up. By the time the workshop folios were completed, children had made a number of significant achievements. They had all tried a number of new writing forms, experimenting with different writing techniques and attempting activities they had not had experience with previously. They had expected that they would be able to succeed with this workshop, and they had. Why?

I think that there were many contributing factors.

1 The children expected to be able to complete the workshop requirements successfully. I had never given them cause to think differently.

2 The children had set the requirements for the workshop — they had chosen the titles they wanted to write about, and therefore they had enjoyed working with these titles.

3 I had ensured that children did not have to write using an unfamiliar writing form. I had demonstrated unknown forms to them, and given them the opportunity to practise them in small or class groups before they were asked to use them by themselves. Children could attempt their work with the confidence of knowing that they had already had some experience with it. Further support from me was on hand if they needed it.

4 The workshop was part of an integrated topic about our society, and the children could see that the information they were researching had relevance to that wider study.

5 They had plenty of time to complete the workshop tasks, even though a deadline had been set. Actually, they enjoyed the challenge of meeting that deadline too!

6 Children knew that an audience had been invited to look at their work — their parents, and friends from other classes — therefore the work was valuable to them, as they wanted to do their best for an audience that was important to them.

All of these factors have to do with the children's expectations.

PART FOUR

FINDING OUT ABOUT LEARNING

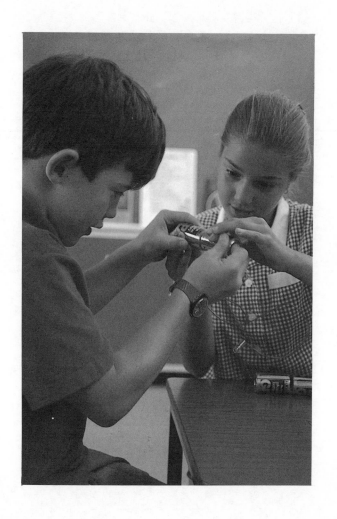

10

FEEDBACK, ASSESSMENT AND REPORTING

◆

I want to know everything I can about the children in my class. I particularly want to know about their learning, because my teaching depends on knowing. Accordingly:

1 Before the school year begins, I plan an assessment program that will give me as much information as possible about children's learning.

2 I organise my classroom routines and procedures to allow information gathering to occur. Assessment of, and response to learning will be based on the information.

3 Finally, but most importantly, from day one of the school year, I observe the children and their learning so that I can understand and assess the responses they need and want, and prepare to meet them.

PLANNING FOR AN EFFECTIVE ASSESSMENT PROGRAM

There are two important factors that I consider when planning an assessment program. Most importantly, however I decide to gather information about children's learning in order to assess that learning, I must base my methods on what I know about:

- how people learn
- the curriculum content and learning processes
- my classroom organisation and working habits

Then I consider time. These days, classroom teachers have little spare time, and certainly none at all within the school day. If I am to assess at all, it must form part of my normal daily routine in the classroom rather than an extra obligation that adds to my teaching load.

CRITERIA FOR CHOOSING INFORMATION-GATHERING AND ASSESSMENT PROCESSES

- Information-gathering and assessment processes must be **part of the normal teach/monitor/evaluate = program cycle**. They must be continuously 'in action', monitoring what is happening at the time it is happening, and responding as necessary.
- They must be **flexible**. They need to cater for each child. Because every child walks a different learning path, they must be adaptable.
- They must be **broad-based**, looking at children and their learning from all angles — what might be the important piece of information that will tell me what the child is doing? I don't know until I've looked at *all* the information.
- Information must be **cumulative**, to be reread and reflected upon:
  ...last month the child could...
  ...yesterday the child discovered...
  ...today it became evident...

  My aim here would be to build up a comprehensive profile of the child's learning.

  Long-term records documenting learning development through all the child's school years would be useful for teachers, the child and parents.
- The information gathering must be **simple** — data collected must be easy to read, to interpret and draw inferences from. Other people — teachers, parents and the child — should be able to read, understand and make responses about the learning from the data.
- The information must contain **input from everyone involved** in the learning, especially the children!
- Above all, the information needs to be used, for **effective** assessment of children's learning.

Children change and develop all the time. If I am to help them to learn effectively, my reactions and responses need to be immediate, helping children know where they have been, where they are now, and where they are going, and giving them strategies for their learning. There is no point spending time collecting information, and then losing sight of the purposes for it.

PURPOSES FOR ASSESSMENT

Who am I assessing for? Who needs this information?

1 THE TEACHER NEEDS THE INFORMATION

I want to clarify my understanding of children's learning, to follow their development and see the processes they are using. I want to monitor their strengths and needs, so that I can tailor the learning programs to suit each child. I want to be able to respond quickly and appropriately so that children can continue their learning development without stops and starts. For example, when I see a child floundering during a reading session, I want to have enough information about that child to be able to say,

> *I know that child is having difficulty choosing appropriate reading material: I will show him the 'five fingers down' method of choosing material to suit his reading abilities,*

or,

> *I know that particular child is bored with that book; it's not an interesting topic for him. I will meet him in the library at lunchtime to choose materials that will interest him.*

2 CHILDREN NEED THE INFORMATION

The children need to clarify their understandings about their learning. They need to have insights into what is happening, to check their progress and see what they have done in order to think logically about what they should do next.

3 THE WHOLE CLASS, AS A GROUP, NEEDS THE INFORMATION

The class needs to know what has happened, why this happened, what they did, what should they do now? What does the group know? What achievements have been made?

Co-operative learning behaviours within the group can only be assessed when the group itself knows what behaviours it has, and what changes might need to be made to those behaviours in order to make learning effective.

4 THE SCHOOL COMMUNITY NEEDS THE INFORMATION

Reporting to parents, teachers and other involved people requires a sound core of useful information to be available.

5 CURRICULUM PLANNING NEEDS THE INFORMATION

I need to know what the children know in order to find where the starting point in the learning program should be, what steps should be planned, what content, what learning processes and skills should be known, and where children are likely to move to next.

I will evaluate the effectiveness of my curriculum in terms of children's interaction with it and their learning development within it.

ASSESSMENT INFORMATION

What information needs to be collected for assessment and response? What do I need to find out about?

Firstly, I want to know what the children know about the **content** of the topics they have been studying.

- Have they learned the facts with which they have been working? For example, in a study of frogs, do they now know that frogs need water and insects in order to live?
- Have they extended their ideas about these facts? For example, do they now understand that frogs are dependent on an environment where their needs will be met?
- Have they made any generalisations based on the facts? For example, have they transferred their specific knowledge about frogs to other animals, and realised that all animals are dependent on their environments?
- Have they formed any theories based on the facts? For example, do they now perceive that all living things are dependent on their environment, and that environments themselves are interdependent?

Secondly, I want to know what **learning skills** children have acquired, how effective these are, and what strategies for learning they are developing?

- Have they developed information-gathering skills and mastered techniques of:
    researching
    observing
    tabling
    classifying
    exploring
    investigating
    collecting
    identifying
    listing
- Have they developed thinking and evaluative skills?
    questioning
    analysing
    inferring
    interpreting
    comparing and contrasting
    predicting
    generalising
    reflecting
    assessing
    explaining
- Have they developed social skills?
    sharing information
    contributing
    co-operating

taking turns
participating
responsibility
flexibility
independence
- Have they developed specific, formal learning processes and skills?
planning
constructing
recording
using and presenting information
discussing, speaking, debating
listening
writing
reading
computing
spelling
editing,
etc.

COLLECTING THE INFORMATION

In order to collect all the information I need to assess children's learning, I use many collection methods. I collect information from the whole class, from small groups, from individuals, and from children's own assessment records.

BRAINSTORMING FOR INFORMATION OR...WHAT DO YOU KNOW NOW?

Throughout a unit of work, I monitor whole class learning by having the children talk about their work during periodic discussion sessions.

These sessions are particularly helpful when the topic is to do with developing children's social behaviours, particularly co-operative learning skills. Children can begin to analyse their behaviours by 'talking through' them, by listening to others in the group interpreting them differently, by forming opinions about ways to behave differently and by predicting possible changes they could make and the effect this would have on group behaviour.

Typically, I would ask for statements of understanding about the topic at several different stages through the unit.

1 At the beginning of the unit, maybe just after an initial shared experience that had focused attention on the topic.

For example, I felt that children in a Year 8 group needed to become aware of the social pressures within their group. They were a discordant group, who found it difficult to work together in co-operative ways. There were a number of leaders in the group who used their popularity to manipulate their followers into displaying unsocial behaviours. In fact, at times it was gang warfare!

A unit of work looking at popularity began with a shared session listening to the music of favourite pop groups. When the whole class listed their ideas about 'What makes pop groups popular?', they revealed a high degree of awareness of the complexity of pop group popularity.

looks shows songs music type of message Variety of songs

image FILM CLIPS quality of recording air play

P.R marketing WHAT MAKES POP GROUPS POPULAR? concerts people

record company dress they're with Commercial advertising

fashion where they are from — eg country

BEHAVIOUR ON STAGE

peer group pressure 'comeback' groups number of RECORDS

instruments used

Class list: What makes pop groups popular?

2 After several sessions looking at the topic further, for example, popularity of people in sport, the media, and in literature, children were asked to write down, individually, their responses to the question, 'What do you have to do to be popular?' Their work showed that most children were working with their own specific and personal observations of popularity to answer this question.

We needed to work on the topic further, so that children could begin to be objective in their opinions.

Popularity is ... being popular!

The people I know who are popular have some good looks, great personality and just are fun to be with.

Where as others really show-off and swear to show that they're so tough when they're not.

Sometimes I feel really daggy because I'm not as popular but in a way I'm glad, because the more popular you are, the more people look at you, and maybe even say bad things behind your back.

Now for the pop group popularity!
I think its the way they present themselves and their songs.
Looks count too, but my favorite band isn't that good looking!
But the songs are ace!
So being popular can be handy, but in a way you might get sick of it!

(Get what I mean?)

___

Popularity is...(Ann)

3 Towards the conclusion of the unit, we looked for generalisations about popularity. For example, after further sessions investigating popular and unpopular characters in literature, children were asked to share their ideas about popularity in small, randomly appointed groups. Some generalisations were made by groups, showing a move from previous specific understandings.

During these sessions, I had also observed children's social interactions in and out of the classroom to see whether they had begun to reach different understandings about their group's behaviour as a result of this work unit. For example:

• Were they aware of the reasons why particular members of the group were popular? Their final lists showed that they had become very aware of these.

POPULARITY IS ...

When something or somebody is popular because of their bodies, personality, clothes, etc.

... Being able to take a joke and not too afraid to make a fool of themselves.
... Being able to live up to the expectations of others.
... Supporting friendships and standing by your word.
... Being by your friend's side when they need you most.
... Being able to understand other's problems and viewpoints.
... Being the best at something which eveyone else admires.

A pop group becomes famous because they have good looks, they're cool
and groovy. It is the same with school kids. Some bully in the school can be
popular by bashing up people with gangs. Smart ass kids in the school are
the same. They use their mouths too much and get popularity that way. They
make other kids feel bad, down in the dumps, maybe even like they want to
kill themselves.

Popularity is...(group list)

- Were there differences in the way they responded to popular
  members of the group? Yes: they were afraid of the 'bully', admiring
  and envious of the beauty, an audience for the clown.
- Because of what they were learning about popularity, were some
  people, popular before these sessions, now losing popularity? Yes:
  the group bully was now obviously losing power over the group, and
  as a result, he was changing his behaviour.

This information formed part of my assessment of their social
behaviour as a group and guided the response I made to the group.
My response took the form of follow-up activities which aimed at
increasing individual children's self-esteem and developing the group's
co-operative behavioural skills.

Our dragon grap is going To show all there Things, To The grade and mrs gordon We have got Lisa doing a book darren doing a wall Poster. Jason is doin a Picher of a dragon and We have all got our heads Together

Lisa's observations

Children themselves are very astute at observing their own behaviour. They are usually honest and realistic about what they are doing, and can describe their own behaviour accurately. Here is Lisa, discussing what is happening in the group with which she is working, and describing the organisation and working behaviours she has observed. We can tell that Lisa herself is a responsible group worker — 'We have all got our heads together,' she says.

COLLECTING INFORMATION FROM INDIVIDUAL CHILDREN

COLLECTING WORK SAMPLES
Looking at children's products provides sure evidence of their learning. What does Lukas know about life cycles?

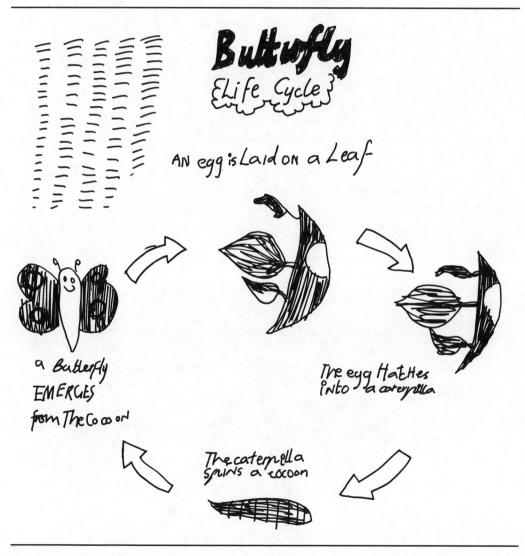

Work sample (Lukas)

◆

What does Tegan know about life cycles?

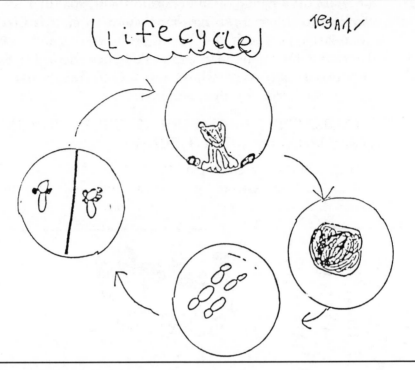

Work sample (Tegan)

What has Jed learned about life cycles?

The Caterpillar
Written by Jed.

One day I saw a caterpillar laying eggs
on a stinging nettle leaf and two months
later the baby caterpillar came out of the
eggs.

Ten months later they spun their chrysalis.
Then 635 butterflies came out of the
chrysalis.

Work sample (Jed)

Each of these children was involved in the same unit of work, and obviously they have learnt different things from it. It is important for me to know this, especially when further work on the topic is being planned.

What does David know about 'The Phantom'? Just about everything there is to know, as is obvious in his retelling of an introductory description from the preface of the comic series.

The Legend Of The Phantom

Phantom comics have been around since 1936. The first one appeared as a syndicated strip in American daily newspapers on 17 febuary 1936. The Phantom colors are purple and black, plus a bit of white in his pants. The sighn of the phantom is 💀e his good mark is this. Lee Falk created Phantom Comics and some people who draw them are

Roger Moore and Sg Barry. They are up to number 949 now. The Phantom lives in the Skull Cave and has a Tree House Castle in the air. He has got a wolf called Devil and horse called hero his wife is Diana

He has two kids called Kit and Heliouse and a froster son called Rex His worst enemy is the singh Pirates. People who wear his goald Mark are always protected by the Phantom. The Pygmy Bandat People protect the skull Cave.

They are the most feared tribe in the jangle Gwan is their leader and is a good friend of the phantom. People say the phantom did not die. Realy it is passt on to his oldest son, The current Phantom is the 21st phantom who became the phantom when his father the 20th Phantom passed it on to him.

Work sample (David)

COLLECTING INFORMATION ABOUT WRITING

Detailed information about children's learning can be collected during conference sessions. During a language session, I would normally have a number of different types of conferences. It is important contact time and a way of keeping tabs on:

- each child's language development
- each child's progress through a learning process, for example, the writing process stages of pre-writing, drafting and editing.
- programming to cater for individual needs

Of course, it would be impossible to hold lengthy conferences with every child every day, but a daily routine and a flexible timetable allows me to be aware of what each child is doing each day.

WRITING CONFERENCES

To help me keep informed about children's writing, I use several different types of writing conference.

The roving conference

As the children settle down to write during a language session, I wander about, quickly checking that all children are on task and that they know what they are doing next. I make sure that they have the resources they need. I ask a few questions, take a few mental notes, jot down a few written notes in my diary, answer a few questions. This is my **roving conference**, and I may have two or three of these 'quick conferences' during a language session, checking and trouble shooting.

The group conference

I spend ten to fifteen minutes of each language session with a **group conference**. All children are rostered to a group, and each group is rostered to a day, so that children would know that Tuesday, for instance, was their group conference day, and they could prepare for this session. At these conferences, children can discuss their writing to date, getting feedback from me and from the other children in the group.

I take notes on work in progress, concerns, needs, in my diary.

There are advantages to having constant group members — children can relax, they are among people who know them well, and who know the work in progress from the previous conference session.

There is also an unspoken law in my class that death is preferable to the consequences of coming uninvited to a group conference and interrupting proceedings. It is important that the session is not disturbed, as children need to be able to talk through writing hassles they may have without losing their train of thought.

Individual conferences

Each day, not necessarily during specific language sessions, I would have two or three **individual conferences** with children. A conference

WRITING ANALYSIS SHEET	
TITLE _____ YEAR LEVEL _____ STUDENT _____ DATE _____	
WRITING CHALLENGES	TEACHER COMMENTS
1. IDEAS title; procedures which lead to choice pre-writing organisation e.g. note-taking, character devel drawing influence for writing e.g. other books, TV show ownership; e.g. paraphrase	
2. STORY ORGANISATION writing type; e.g. personal narrative opening; introduction sequence; development ending; effective clear main idea; focus clear to reader	
3. LANGUAGE suited to reader? suited to story? adding mood to action feelings emphasis personal style? uses descriptive language; e.g. similes, adjectives, book lang.	
4. MECHANICS spelling; graphonic? other strategies? punctuation paragraphs apostrophes, dialogue	
5. PRESENTATION/HANDWRITING mechanics; formation, shape, size, slant, spacing aesthetics speed	
NOTES: with reference back to previous writing analysis sheets, new developments, new understandings, strategies used information conveyed	

Writing analysis sheet

♦

list is by my table, and children can write their names on it if they require an individual conference during any stage of their writing. I keep fairly detailed records of these conferences, using a writing analysis sheet to give me a clear picture of what the child is doing.

I keep the writing analysis sheets filed under a cover sheet so that I also have a quick summary of the child's writing history as a 'ready reference'.

NAME: *Lisa*

WRITING DEVELOPMENT.

DATE	INFORMATION AND STRATEGIES USED.
Feb 88	Storyline- imaginative episodic, 3 pages long Language - sentence structure good, random use of capital letters. Spelling skills developed - probs:- adding - ed, lau(gh)ed, turned end Maybe uses words which she feels she can spell rather than for story making.
2/3/88	Care Bear story — fantasy narrative self correction v.g. problems with plot control — conference this
April	Started using talking marks.
May	Produced parody of "The Jolly Postman" using envelopes, pop-ups etc
July 88	Non-fiction directional "How To Make a Pap. up" used diagrams to explain sequence. Used directional language used pap-ups themselves to demonstrate Using author's page in publishing.
11·8·88	New story "The Zoo" S.C. Chapter!
Sept	Chp 12!?! of "The Zoo". Conference to

Writing cover sheet

Sharing conferences

At the end of each language session, I call a whole class **sharing conference**. At these conferences, the children share their successes and celebrate their completed work. They may ask for criticism or offer help in editing. They discuss whole class or group publishing projects.

This is a useful way of allowing children to see what others are doing, and to reflect on what they themselves have been doing. They can respond positively to what they like about each other's work. I can demonstrate appropriate responses. Children can hear me respond to a classmate's work by praising specific instances of achievement, for example, 'The way you started your story by saying "You won't believe this, but my house is haunted" really made me keen to read on. What an interesting story starter! Where did you get the idea?'

During this conference, I continue to jot down any useful information about children's learning in my diary.

Daily diary: sample page

Daily diary

I use this diary to record notes about children as events occur, not only during writing, but at *all* times during the day. It's easy and simple to carry about, and is a great aid to the teacher who finds his/her memory a poor frail thing that is fading fast.

I use an exercise book for my diary. I cut about five centimetres from the edge of all the pages except the first and the last. On these I put the names of the children, half down the outside of the first page and the rest down the outside of the last page. Each double page is then edged with the names of all the children in the class, and is used to jot down notes about them in the two or three lines allowed for each child. Each double page is used for a week's jottings and is a good record of the day-to-day happenings in the classroom. It's easy to see from this record which children are having troubles with a particular aspect of their work, and I can respond to this with immediate programming for those children.

COLLECTING INFORMATION ABOUT READING

I keep informed of children's reading development by using a variety of information-collecting methods.

RUNNING RECORDS

At the beginning of the school year, I usually take a **running record** of each child's oral reading, and continue to monitor children's reading throughout the year by this means.

READING ANALYSIS

In some cases, I spend quite a lot of time with children to assess their reading more accurately. I begin with a running record of their oral reading, and record the results on an analysis sheet. I can see clearly what reading strategies they are depending on, and what they need to develop.

READING INTERVIEWS

To determine what children think about their reading, I conduct reading interviews with them. This also helps me to make my teaching more explicit. What cueing strategies are children aware of? What do they like to read? What do they think a good reader does to become a good reader?

DATE: 18·3·91   STUDENT: Anna

TITLE: The Trouble with Mum

	G.PH.	SYN.	SEM.	COMMENT
✓ ✓ ✓ ✓				
✓ ✓ ✓				
✓ ✓ ✓ ✓				
✓ ✓				
✓ the‾⌐SC / R ✓ ✓ mm/other / TT R			/ /	lost meaning
✓ ✓ ✓ ✓ ✓ ✓				
‾she⌐TF R ✓ ✓ ✓ ✓ R now/new⌐SC R ✓	/	/	/	
✓ ✓ ✓ ✓ ✓ ✓ R				check after losing meaning in previous line.
✓ ✓ ✓ ✓				
✓ keep/kept ✓ ✓ ✓ ✓ ✓ ✓	/			
✓ ✓ ✓ R staying‾SC ✓			/	
✓ ✓ ✓ ✓ ✓ ✓ ✓				

COMMENTS

Uses graphophonic cues
Self corrects for meaning
Reads with some expression that is appropriate for meaning, awareness of listener.
Coped well with difficult text

Sample running record

READING ANALYSIS SHEET

TITLE: YEAR LEVEL:

STUDENT: DATE:

Ask the child to select a book that s/he believes s/he can read. Take a running record of the reading. Record observations of the way the child read in the following summary list

Uses the title
Uses pictorial cues to aid prediction
Demonstrates reading for a purpose (info. enjoyment)
Expects the print to make sense
Actively searches for meaning
Selects key visual information

Use of semantics:
Self corrects when meaning is lost
Makes predictions using meaning
Re-reads to regain meaning
Reads on to gain meaning

Use of syntax:
Self corrects inappropriate language
Predicts using knowledge of language
Re-reads
Reads on

Use of graphophonics:
Uses grapho-phonics information to aid prediction
Uses initial letter or letters
Reads word by word
Relies on phonics to work out an unknown word
Uses grapho-phonics regardless of meaning
(e.g. The house galloped by)

Comments:
with reference back to previous reading analysis sheets. New developments, new understandings, strategies used.

Suitabiltiy of text?

Can retell with meaning/accuracy

Reading analysis sheet

Name: Emma 27/5

Reading interview

Do you like reading?

Yes

What do you read?

All sorts. I like reading everything. I don't
like science fiction or horror much.

When you are reading and you come to something you don't
know, what do you do?

I try to understand by reading it over.
I ask someone.

Do you ever do anything else?

Sound it out.

Who is a good reader that you know? James
Leah

What makes them a good reader?

They read good books. They're not put off
if the book looks hard.

Do you think they ever come to something they don't know when
they are reading?

Yes

What do you think they do?

The same sorts of things I do I think.

If you kew someone was having trouble with reading, how
would you help?

I'd ask them what they didn't know, help
understand meanings of words, ask them to sound

What would your teacher do to help?   it out.

Ask them to remember where they'd seen or heard
it before.

What would you like to do to be a better reader?

read more variety
try more challenging books

Emma's reading interview

Emma is aware of several reading cues: graphophonic (I sound it out), visual memory (remember where [I've] heard or seen it before), rereading to check meaning (I try to understand by reading it over). She likes to read all sorts of reading materials, but not science fiction or horror. Because she sees good readers as people who are prepared to persevere with a book even 'if the book is hard', she will be most likely to do this herself. She wants to be a better reader and 'try more challenging books', just like the good readers she sees.

READING AND RETELLING

The information that can be gathered from this one sample of work is amazing.

How it works

A short piece of text is selected to be read. The choice of text is influenced by the children in the class, and by the work being done in the classroom at the time. At the time that Natalie read this sample text, the class was investigating the reasons people have had for coming to Australia.

Step one: predicting content

The title of the text is read to the children, and then displayed. Children are asked to write one or two sentences predicting the content of the text, using the title as a clue. Then they are asked to write a list of words they think might be contained in a text with this title. They discuss their predictions with others in small discussion groups, and are encouraged to tell each other why they have made the predictions they have.

Step two: reading the content

The teacher then reads the entire text to the whole group, to demonstrate how a good reader reads this text. Finally, children are given the text to read by themselves. They can read it as many times as they wish in order to feel confident that they understand the text.

Step three: paraphrasing the content

Then they are asked to retell the content in their own words, without reference to the text. This part can be oral or written. There are advantages in having written retellings: some assessment can be made of children's writing skills as well. Proofreading is encouraged.

Step four: checking understanding of content

After the time limit is up, usually ten to fifteen minutes, children are asked to find a partner with whom they can share and compare their retellings. They look at similarities and differences between the two

READING AND RETELLING.

NAME of STUDENT: Natalie Vella

TITLE: Safe in Australia,

What do you think this book/article/story will be about?

how people migrate to Australia and how there are no wars in Australia and how people are basically safe from wars and things

What words might be used?   Write a list.

migrate
safe
Australia
wars
away
migrant

Retell the book/ article/story.

Its about a war in Vietnam and a family living there they leave the mother and daughter and leave on a ship with 193 other people trying to escape they are leaving for Australia they are very desperate and thirsty and are only allowed one or two drops of water a day and drunk each others urine they are so desperat to cool of, they bathe in the sea but they relise it is dangerouse because of sharks. One day they thought a shark would overturn the boat they thought their blood attracted it from their dry lips. They saw a ship in the distance and as it came closer they saw it was a pirate ship but they didn't attack because it was 193 again. they met a fisherman and swapped Gold for food water and petrol. at last they came to malaysia and the very drunk so much water he had a stomahe ache

---

Natalie's read and retell

retellings, and the strengths and weaknesses of each. This part of the procedure is the most important, as it enables children to look critically at their work, in a reasonably non-threatening and private way. They are asked to make statements about their work, and to give reasons for their statements. They can look closely at the text and see that there is more than one way to interpret it.

Using reading and retelling as an assessment procedure
Teachers can collect a lot of information about the children's reading from these retellings:

- Can children predict what the content might be?
- What vocabulary might be included?
- Do children understand the content of what they read?
- Have they understood the main idea?
- Do they use their own words in their retelling, or the author's?
- Do they appreciate the author's intentions, the unspoken message?
- Have they focused on the author's use of language?
- Can they identify the author's style?
- Can they reflect on what they have gained by the reading?

Of course, all these questions are not likely to be answered in one read and retell session. Other questions, not asked here, may be answered instead. Some of the questions may be dealt with during the post-reading discussion, and not recorded.

Natalie was asked to predict what an article titled 'Safe in Australia' might be about. She predicted that it would be about Australia's freedom from warfare, and how desirable this would be from a migrant's point of view. When she read the article, she would have discovered that her prediction was correct. Her summary of the article has included the author's main ideas; she has mentioned some of the more important details; she has not mentioned the underlying current of fear for life, and grief at family separation, the inferences of 'last and only chance'.

In my assessment of Natalie's reading performance, I can conclude that:

- she is using her background knowledge to predict accurately
- she reads for meaning
- she can summarise in a clear and logical manner
- she has yet to develop her abilities to make inferences from the text.

I can also make some assessment of her writing from this same sample of work.

COLLECTING INFORMATION FROM CHILDREN'S SELF-ASSESSMENT

I always expect children to participate in their own assessment. In fact, the more involved children become in the assessment of their own learning, the better they can come to terms with their own abilities, skills, strengths and weaknesses.

READING DIARIES

Children keep their own record of what they have read. From this list, we can see what types of literature children like to read, what reading level they feel comfortable with, and how much they read.

NAME Alexander

DATE	BOOK:title	COMMENTS
May 24	Blooding	Very good book
26	Eighteenth Emergency	Not the best
30	TV Kid	funny book
June 4	Blinky Bill	very adventurous
7	Ginger Meggs	Comedy
21	King Arther and the round table	
30	The witches	Exciting
July 3	superfudge	Funny
7	Hating Alison Ashley	Funny
11	Space Demons	Excellent

Reading diary (Alexander)

PERSONAL DIARIES

I expect children to keep personal diaries. They are asked to record anything about school that they feel is important to them. Every so often I ask them to answer specific questions about their learning. These diaries serve two purposes:

- they create a personal record for the children so that they can review and respond to their own development
- the teacher has the opportunity to respond to children's personal tastes, interests, and comments in a fairly private exchange with the child

Sometimes I ask the children to address a focus question in their diary: 'Have you written a diary before, either as a personal record or as a story for publication? Have you read any books written as diaries?'

I've tried writing in Diary form but I've found it hard becuse it's something that I wouldn't want to share with anyone because when I write a Diary, I write about mysef so it might be persenal. But I'd like people to read it later on, maybe. I like true sounding Diaries or sad and happy ones. I hate scifi books. I think they sound babyish. I read alot at home and I really enjoy it. Please comment. I don't know whether Anne Frank meant people to read her diary; I think

Personal diary entry (CL)

'What did you think of our first class meeting? What would you do to improve the way we run it?'

be fun, and A great expereince for all of us I hope to go to MP.C next year

Dear Diary,
I think we should learn to listen to others and not to make unesseary comments, And for the punishments to be given
Dear Diary We were use to starting off

Personal diary entry (CKL)

If children want me to reply to their diary entries, they must ask. They write 'please comment' at the end of their diary entry, and I always accept the invitation. It's a good chance to provide some specific and personal information for children to reflect on.

LEARNER QUESTIONNAIRES

Periodically, I ask the children to think about themselves as writers, or readers, and to fill in a questionnaire detailing information about their learning.

Here are Ozgul's answers to a reading questionnaire.

NAME: *Ozgul*

1. **What helps you choose the books you read?**
   List sources, influences, etc.

   The back cover.
   Flicking through pages and reading small parts of book.

2. **List some of the books that you have really enjoyed reading recently.**

   She's a Rebel   *First Impressions*
   Summer Escape   *She's Got the Best*
   Stroke of Luck   *In Too Deep*

3. **Who are your favorite authors?**

   — mixed

4. **What type of stories/books do you enjoy reading best of all?**
   eg., mystery, fantasy, romance, factual etc.

   Romance — it's just a phase I'm going through.

5. **How often do you read?**   Daily?   Weekly?   Sometimes?
   How much time do you spend reading?

   Daily, 6 hours, and any other free time.
   4.00 to 6.00pm and then 10.00 to 12.00 pm

Reading questionnaire (Ozgul)

From her answers, I can see that I should offer her books to read that will move her gently away from romance and into more substantial reading. It won't be a difficult task, as she is obviously a voracious reader who is well aware of her reading habits.

James is answering questions about his writing.

WRITING INTERVIEW

Name: James

Do you enjoy writing?

Yes.

What do you do when you can't think of anything to write? I go to someone and & ask them for ideas and look

Do you ever do anything else? At books.

No

What do you do if you are having some difficulty with your writing? I go back and read what I've written so I know what comes next.

Who are some good writers you know, and what makes them good writers?

Danae because she always thinks of the story first and writes them

Do you think they ever have any difficulty with their writing?

Yes

What do they do about it? They read what they have written already.

How would you help someone having difficulty with their writing?

I would read their stories and give them ideas to write from there.

What would you like to do to be a better writer?

I would read more books so I know how other people write stories.

Writing questionnaires (James)

Writing questionnaires provide information about children's writing, particularly this type, which looks at the strategies children use to choose topics for writing. Knowing what topics children like to write about will help the teacher to plan for support groups for writing and to guide future study of different writing forms.

WRITE YOUR OWN REPORT

Each term I ask the children to discuss their learning for that term. I ask them to write down as much information as possible. Ozgul, in Year 8, lists her achievements:

NAME *Ozgul Cinar*

Discuss what you have achieved in your English Language work this term. Talk about your reading and writing, and any talks, debates, etc., in which you have been involved.

In English this term & the one before we have done stories on sci-fi, which I dislike.
We read the book called Pigman by Paul Zindel. After that I read another 5 books of his. He's a great author! This year I was involved in 2 debates. One was on Nuclear weapons, which should be produced and Marijuana should be banned. Our side won both of them. It was great fun!

Self-assessment (Ozgul)

Lee, in Year 6, found that 'nothing was easy'.

MY LEARNING IS GOING GOOD SO FAR
I've enjoyed this week and I hope next week is just the same.
SLam was O.K I found some of the special school kids a little bit odd but ok Magic squares was hard but I found that not much was easy. I think I did o.K with my folio but I think I could do better at mechanics in my stories.

Self-assessment (Lee)

◆

I have never found children to be dishonest in their self-assessments; on the contrary, they are extremely frank and conscientious, and they have a very clear idea about what they are doing, and where they plan to work next. Their assessments directly feed into program planning for themselves and for others in their class. Their assessments also contribute to reporting.

REPORTING TO OTHERS

When I am reporting to others on children's learning, I use all the information gathered within my classroom to write about and discuss each child.

This is an end-of-year report on Alexander's progress. Reports like these can be written each term.

MOONEE PONDS CENTRAL SCHOOL No. 8565
STUDENTS CONFIDENTIAL REPORT

June 19 _89_

Name _Alexander_   Term 1 ②3 4

Level _8_   Subject _English Language_ Interim 1 2 3 4

Alexander has satisfactorily completed the following tasks.

1. He has written two pieces of personal writing, both showing that he understands the narrative form of story structure. He uses conventional spelling, structure and grammar.

2. He has produced some directed writing in class-characterisations, 'haiku' poetry, retellings of short stories and poetry- where his presented work demonstrates his writing competence. He has a clear understanding of authors intentions which is reflected in his comprehension of their writing. He shows an appreciation of his audience in his own writing.

3. Alexander has read and participated thoughtfully in class, discussion of two novels- 'The Pigman' and 'Grinny'. He regularly reads factual texts, and would benefit by reading more fiction.

4. He has presented a short talk to his classmates, on a topic of personal interest, and he has participated as the whip in a class debate. His team won the day largely due to Alexander's ability to sum up his team's key issues and to produce convincing argument against the opposition's.

    Alexander contributes to all English language lessons. His contributions are valued by others.

Alexander's end-of-year report

I make my written reports as anecdotal as possible, obviously 'celebrating' achievements and developments. Children are free to add or delete information if they have a sound basis for doing so, just as I must have a sound basis for the information I write in a report.

Some reporting is done informally: children write in class and school newspapers and newsletters.

Year Six have been reading and writing Italian recipes during their Italian sessions. This week they had-a-go at cooking an Italian recipe during their nutrition session, in Italian, of course!

On Tuesday we made pizzas. We had to read the recipe in Italian. We were divided into groups and each group made one or two pizzas. In the morning we made the dough and left it to rise. Then we pulled it into shape, and added the toppings - mushrooms, tomato puree, black olives, ham, salami, capsicum, cheese. Then we cooked it. Ours was a bit doughy, but it was good. It was much better than I thought it would be!

Danielle.

Photo albums, class books, videos and letters detailing class events, class work and activities are taken home to show parents, put in the school library for others to read, borrowed by other classes, and used to report on class and individual products and progress whenever and wherever possible. Children's products are displayed, shared, spoken about, advertised, used for their purposes.

Have I collected the information I need in order to be able to assess children's learning? Have my collection and method of assessment met my initial criteria? Yes:

- it has been part of the normal daily classroom routine at all times
- it has been flexible, providing many ways of looking at children's learning
- it is certainly broad-based, looking at the children and their learning from all angles
- it has given me an accumulation of documentation about each child
- all the documentation is simple to read and interpret — a child could do it, and they mostly do!
- information has come from everyone involved with the children, and especially the children themselves
- it has been efficient — there is no unused information collected, all of it has been directly related to the present and future learning of the children, detailing what they are doing, and what responses need to be made to continue their learning.

CONCLUSIONS

BRINGING IT ALL TOGETHER

When do you know that the children in your class are learning?

1 When they know what they are doing.

I am writing this book for my little brother. It's another adventure story about Thomas the Tank Engine because that's his favourite.

2 When they can tell you the purposes they have for the learning and they have decided for themselves what those purposes are.

Can I borrow your book about space? I want to know more about rocket launches for my story.

3 When they know what they need to learn and they have set goals to fulfil those needs.

I am practising writing the alphabet today.

4 When they get help when they need it.

Will you show me how to put in the talking marks?

5 When they are prepared to watch demonstrations of how to do the things they want to learn.

Are you going to show us how to write recipes today?

6 When they like to practise.

How come we haven't done any writing yet this morning?

7 When they monitor and respond to their learning progress, to see what they need to learn next, and when they have several strategies for this.

◆

- They recognise their errors, and work to correct them.

Today I handed in my folio. I think I
went all right. But the best parts
are my title page and my contents
and also my stories. The good points
are my sheets that I did in
class. The parts that could be better
are my front cover. But I tried
to do it. And also my writing. I would
assess my self by writeing about my

Leah talks about her latest piece of work, and reflects on her performance.

- They gain confidence from their successes.

November 8, 1990.

Dear Parents,

You are invited to visit Years 5 and 6 classrooms on Monday November-ber 12 (5.30pm - 7.00pm) to see an exhibition of work by students in Years 5 and 6.

    The exhibition, called:

        A Great Week, October 22nd - 26th

        •Canberra Camp

        •The Alternative Camp

is well worth seeing!

   Videos made during this week will be shown in the Library from 6.00 pm. Refreshments will be served.

Dale Gordon
Kevin Gardiner
Years 5 and 6 Teachers.

Here, parents are invited to share success with their children. The invitation lets children know that others, their teachers, also consider that they were successful in their work.

- They compare their opinions about their own learning with the opinions of their peers, to see whether their view of their learning is similar. Learners who know their own strengths and weaknesses can assume responsibility for learning what they need to know in order to progress.

WORKSHOP DIARY SHEET.   NAME: Emma Valente

TITLE	DATE, COMMENT	NAME
The Greatest danger of summer	7.2.90 well written, great message for all ages	Leah . M
Its better to be safe then sorry.	20/2/90 It was a really good story	Alison
"	21.2 Ready to publish	Jordan
Classwork	Fire Safety diagrams are a little unclear. All classwork has been completed.	
25.2. Emma,	Spelling: story → stories	
	You have completed all the requirements for this workshop. Work has been competently produced and well presented. Did you do your own typing? It was very proficient. Your own assessment of your work is accurate. How would (will) you change the way you use time next workshop? Can you think of ways you could be more efficient? Your 'Greatest Danger of Summer' story certainly deserved to be published in the school newsletter.	
		Rej.

PRESENTATION OF FOLIO: Your presentation was a little haphazard — but when it was good it was very, very good!

Emma's friends offer her opinions and advice on her writing

- They work with others in co-operative groups. Their learning can be supported by the group generally in unobtrusive and non-threatening ways. Learners who feel comfortable with their learning tasks because of the security of the group support engage with those learning tasks confidently.

YESTERDAY, YEAR 6 had a nutrition session. We ate submarines (rolls split in half, and baked with a delicious topping of tomato, salami and grated cheese) and lettuce cup salads, followed by fruit salad.

We drank apple fruit juice sodas. These recipes were invented by 2 of our class members - Chonet Adams and David Brown-Welsh. We thought the submarines were the best.

Probably most of the class would agree. The class was divided into groups and each group prepared one item for the rest of us.

Our thanks to group 4 who did the clearing and washing up.

Darren Tsang and Ben Levett.

Here, Ben and Darren write about a cooking session for the school newsletter. It is clear from their description of this class activity that everyone in the class contributed to the success of the session. Some class members — Chonet, David and the children in 'group four' — would feel valued and successful because of their special mention, and this would most likely influence their future learning and participation in group work.

- They reflect on their progress and evaluate their performance. They can see the directions their learning needs to take, and can begin to take those steps.

What are the characteristics of the teacher who is engaging children in their learning?

I am aware of what the children need to learn.
Each learning experience may have a different purpose for the child, but the underlying understanding is the same — the learning occurs because it is needed, future decisions and actions depend on it. It is important that I make this explicit for the children. I want them to know that the learning they do in my classroom will have a purpose for them that will affect their future learning.

The learning will be in response to the needs, interests and concerns of each individual learner.

I understand how they need to go about their learning.
- I demonstrate learning behaviours.
- I discuss purposes and methods for learning.
- I try to help children become aware of what they do when they are learning, so they can repeat it.
- I allow children to plan their learning.

13/9/90   My Project   Dear Diary
I started with more than enough Information
and got my research out of the way fairly quickly
I found the hard (it organising my work
I spent too long on that and therefor my
Presentation/didit have or much time as i
would have liked on it.
　　　　　I had planned re do a model
but again I left it too late Next time I'm going
re write up time table to help me.
　　　　　I'm also going to get the book Looks grea'
which will help me.
　　　　　Over all I thought it was a fairly average
project   All the steps took a long time and I
spent too much time on them, took then to

James reviews his work on a project. He sees where he needs to take action: time management — '(I'll) write up a timetable to help me'; resources — 'I'm also going to get the book "Looks Great", which will help me.'

- I expect children to learn in ways that are best for them.
- I encourage co-operative learning groups, knowing that peer teaching is powerful.
- I allow time for review and reflection so that children can monitor their learning, and assess and evaluate their progress.

I understand that there are many parts to my role.

- I create the learning environment that allows the children to learn. One experience after another must build up into positive attitudes about learning and the learner.
- I ensure that learning experiences are linked, so that children can see a natural learning path.
- I monitor, assess and report on each child's learning.
- I assess my own performance.
- I evaluate my program.
- **I remember that I too am a learner**. I must be in control of my own learning and recognise the same self-improving system operating within myself that I want to see in the children around me.

Will children always be learning? Probably yes, but not always what I think they will be learning that day! In practical terms, I must be aware of the learning that is present without my intention, and that is not a conscious part of my well-orchestrated classroom planning. For instance, I cannot expect the class to be following the planned program when they have just had the unexpected opportunity to see the stage play of *Hating Alison Ashley* put on by a neighbouring school, and are enthusiastically engrossed in anything written by Robin Klein, to the exclusion of all else. No. It is the time for Robin Klein.

The day that one of the children brings a litter of newborn white mice to class is the day the whole class studies white mice, and perhaps other rodents as well.

I cannot reasonably expect children to be engaged in their readers theatre activities when the bus to take them to the finals of the interschool sports matches will be picking them up in twenty-five minutes. No. That's the time for a discussion about the certainty of predictions and the law of probability, while some of the children check out the sports equipment bags and make sure we've got it all ready to go.

I must seize the moment and be aware of the learning that is most likely to occur at that moment. I must be ready, be flexible, with resources available to meet sudden demands and interests. I must be prepared to drop planned activities in favour of the activity that will most likely produce learning at that time.

I must therefore know that:

- the most important thing is **the learning**

and that

- the conditions for learning that particular thing might never occur again.

INDEX